STRANGERS

— IN THE —

STORM

STRANGERS

— IN THE —

STORM

LOVE AND SURVIVAL ON
MOUNT RAINIER

JARED RUND & DIANE MCKENNEY

Printed in the United States of America.
Library of Congress Control Number: 2018960030
ISBN: 978-1-732857-37-7

This book is dedicated to our loving parents, family, friends, and all those in search of adventure.

TABLE OF CONTENTS

I will lift up my eyes to the mountains—
where does my help come from?

My help comes from the Lord,
the Maker of heaven and earth.

— Psalm 121:1–2 (NIV)

"In every walk with Nature,
one receives far more than he seeks."
— John Muir

CHAPTER
ONE

"Hey—you wanna climb Rainier?"

That's how it all started: a phone call to a couple crazy guys he used to know from work.

Jared Rund wasn't really a mountain climber. He grew up in a suburb north of Chicago, a place that isn't known for its mountain peaks. Its highest elevation is somewhere around 700 feet, and as far as wilderness, it didn't have a lot to offer, except a flat botanic garden, a flat lagoon, and a flat set of forest trails that Jared used for jogging.

But when he was in middle school, his gym teacher, Mr. Hollmaier—a transplant from Fort Collins, Colorado—installed a climbing wall and made it a regular part of his phys-ed curriculum, and Jared got hooked. The teacher took some of the most avid climbers under his wing, helped them train in the summer, and organized a trip for a club called the "Cool Runners" to run, bike, and climb with him in Colorado, to the summit of a peak that stretched 14,000 feet into the sky. It was the first time Jared had seen big mountains, the first time he'd climbed one—and he knew he loved it.

He kept at climbing over the years. He joined a rock-climbing club in college and used the wall at the college gym, but nothing too serious. It was something he did for fun now and then. He liked using his body, and he liked challenging it in as many ways as he could—not only climbing, but also skiing, mountain biking, and pretty much anything else that presented itself as an option. Physical challenges didn't faze him; they excited him. They gave him a chance to test his limits and prove to himself who he was, what he was capable of doing.

But climbing—especially climbing real mountains—wasn't really a part of his life. He had just graduated from the University of Illinois at Urbana-Champaign and was helping a cousin move to the Seattle area. At the end of the summer, he was planning to head to Montgomery, Alabama, to begin active duty in the Air Force. Between now and then, he had a little time to kill, and he wanted to do it the way he loved best: finding the biggest challenge the region had to offer, and meeting it.

As far as challenges go, Mount Rainier certainly fit the bill. At 14,411 feet, it's the tallest mountain in the Pacific Northwest and the fifth tallest in the continental United States, only ninety-four feet lower than California's Mount Whitney. The giant white cone of Rainier dominates the Seattle skyline so singularly that the people in Washington call it, simply, "the Mountain." As if its sheer size weren't dramatic enough, the Mountain is also an active volcano—big enough and close enough to major cities to be considered one of the most dangerous volcanoes in the world.

And it's no easy climb. Rainier juts out of the ground so sharply and steeply, it has a "topographic prominence" of 13,210 feet—the height between its base and its summit, a higher prominence even than K2, the world's second-tallest mountain. Above its tree line, it's covered in thirty-five square miles of ice, capping the mountain with twenty-six distinct glaciers that crack open—sometimes unexpectedly—into long, seemingly bottomless crevasses. Because of the high altitude, the risks of avalanche, and the severe and unpredictable weather, fewer than half the people who attempt to summit the mountain succeed—and each year, a handful of them die.

You'd have to be really brave to want to climb Rainier, or really driven, or really crazy.

That's why Jared called his friend Jon Claussen. Jon was a mountaineer. But Jared and Jon hadn't met through mountain climbing; they'd met through window washing.

Jared's dad was the Chicago district manager at a window-washing company based in northern Illinois, and Jared had been working there with his dad from the time he was five years old. Back then, he couldn't reach very far and the quality of his work was pretty unreliable, so his dad paid him in donut holes and nickels. By the time Jared was in high school, though, his reach and his work ethic had both improved, and his dad was paying much better; it wound up being a pretty good way to make a living. Jared spent summers during high school and college washing windows in Chicago. "You've heard of the Sears Tower?" Jared would ask people who were curious about his job. "I've washed the windows there." He'd watch as their jaws hit the floor before he went on to explain, "It was the gift shop, inside, on the second floor."

Even though he wasn't working on the side of skyscrapers, the work definitely didn't leave room for any fear of heights. Jared got comfortable with placing ladders and going up and down them, reaching with poles in awkward positions out of open windows, climbing onto rooftops and balancing on ledges, hanging on for dear life while stretching for that one hard-to-reach spot.

Jon and his younger brother, Dan, also worked for the window-washing company, though Jared didn't meet them right away since they worked on a separate route. But the company landed a rush job on the Guess retail store in downtown Chicago, a job that needed to begin at 3:00 a.m., but finish before morning rush hour. Jared's dad called in Jon and Dan to help get the job done.

Jon and Dan were different from most of the guys who worked for Jared's dad, whom they affectionately called "Boss." For starters, they were young—around Jared's age—whereas most of his dad's employees were older. But the brothers were different in other ways too. They were from the Pacific Northwest, from a town outside of Seattle, called Duvall, and they were always talking about climbing mountains. Jon had already summited a few peaks in the South American Andes. He had a linguistic-research job that required him to hike throughout Papua New Guinea, and whenever he had free time, he'd grab his backpack and start wandering into the jungle, coming upon waterfalls and strange animals he didn't recognize and, every now and then, an undocumented village of people who had never seen a white man.

Jon was fearless—maybe sometimes a little *too* fearless. His brother, Dan, was quieter and more responsible, though only a little. The two of them had enjoyed many adventures together, and Jon told story after story while they rushed to finish the job at the Guess store before the sun rose.

Jared knew these adventurous brothers were his kindred spirits.

"We should do something together," he said to Jon as they parted ways in the morning. "You know, before we all have girlfriends and jobs and all those things that will take up all our time."

"Okay. How about this weekend?"

Jon had bought a junker Jet Ski for one dollar from some guy back home named Mr. McKenney, and he was eager to try it out. So Jared met up with him and they rode the Jet Ski around Lake Michigan, discovering after a little work that it wasn't quite a junker after all.

A few months later, Jon and Jared decided to go spearfishing on an island off Puerto Rico, camping on the beach and in an old, abandoned building.

No matter how crazy the Claussens were, Jared wanted to keep up—wanted to prove to them and to himself that he *could* keep up. This was the kind of adventurer he wanted to be. This was the kind of life he wanted to live.

But the three of them still hadn't climbed a mountain together.

When Jared called the Claussens to tell them he was visiting Seattle to help his cousin move, there was only one thing he wanted to do: climb Rainier. He'd looked it up before he even arrived, Googling "What is the tallest mountain in Washington?" Jared wasn't the kind of person who wanted to climb the second- or third-tallest mountain in Washington.

But now that he was actually in Seattle, the urge to climb was stronger than ever. The mountain was right there, gigantic on the southeast horizon, every time he turned a corner.

Dan picked up the phone: "Hey, it's lucky you called! I'm planning to go up Mount Rainier next week!"

And that was that.

Jon was out of town on some adventure or another, but Dan was going to climb the mountain with his fiancée, Amber; Jared's cousin, Titus; and a few other old friends.

Now that the climb was becoming a reality, Jared started getting a little nervous.

"I've never climbed on a glacier before," he confessed to his friend.

"Don't worry about it," Dan reassured him. "We'll lend you some gear and show you how to use it. There's nothing to it. Seriously, I know this eleventh-grader who just did it, and if she can, you can too."

Jared rummaged through Dan's garage for the gear he needed, borrowed some from Titus, and rented boots and an ice axe from REI, an outdoor-gear retailer—and they were ready to go.

There are a lot of different ways to the summit of Rainier, but the most popular ones—the safest ones—all start on the mountain's south side, in an area called Paradise. There's a parking area at the Ranger Station, and from there the trail climbs up, basically straight up, from its starting point at 5,420 feet to a base camp called Camp Muir at 10,080 feet, the halfway point to the summit. It's a lot of elevation to gain over a short distance—but on Rainier, this is what counts as the "easy" day. The rest of the way to the summit involves glaciers, flaky rock, winds strong enough to blow you off the mountain, and air that gets thinner with every step.

Camp Muir has a stone hut that was built to offer shelter to the climbers, but when Jared and his friends arrived, the hut was already full, and they were forced to sleep in their tents out in the snow. However, they didn't sleep for long. Dan explained that climbers pushing for the summit start around midnight.

"You want to get over as much of the glacier as you can before the sun starts to warm things up. You might think 'warm' would be a good thing in a place as cold as this—but when the ice starts melting, it also starts falling. And falling ice is not good."

They set out in the dark up the mountain, following a series of little orange flags the guides and rangers had left in the ice to mark the trail. It was hard—hard for every one of them. It was steep and tiring and cold, but what was taking the biggest toll on the team was the altitude.

The higher a person climbs up a mountain, the thinner the air becomes; the climber is literally walking up out of the atmosphere. And with less oxygen in the air, the body's muscles don't respond as well as they would at lower altitude: they get tired faster and they're slower to recover.

But altitude affects people in other ways too. With less air pressure on the outside of the body, the pressure on the inside of the body pushes outward. Think about opening a water bottle on an airplane and having it hiss and spray from the pressure, or uncapping a pen in the middle of a flight to discover the ink has been squeezed out of it. A version of this same thing happens inside the body, and it can hit climbers hard. Acute Mountain Sickness (AMS) can feel like the flu, or a horrible hangover; it includes terrible headaches, nausea, and vomiting. At its worst, AMS can be life-threatening because it can cause the brain, lungs, and heart to swell, making climbers weak, confused, and/or delirious—or worse.

Climbing too high too fast and ignoring the effects of doing so can kill you.

AMS doesn't affect all climbers equally, but there's no predicting whom it will strike or when. Physical conditioning and drinking lots of water can help stave it off—but the only sure way to prevent altitude sickness is to let your body acclimate to the thin air gradually by spending days at altitude. Once a climber starts feeling the effects of AMS, it's already too late. The symptoms won't go away on their own; the only "cure" is to get to a lower altitude immediately.

A few members of Jared's team were already feeling the effects of the thin air. The team had started in Duvall, Washington, eighty-nine feet above sea level—and now they were climbing up around 12,000 feet. They soldiered on as well as they could, but many of them were suffering from headaches and nausea. They made it as far as Little Tahoma, a steep peak of crumbling rock that cuts up above the clouds on the way to the true summit, and stayed long enough to watch the sunrise.

But then they conceded that they were going to have to turn around. They wouldn't be summiting Rainier after all.

They took the long trek down the mountain, quiet in their disappointment. Jared kept looking back over his shoulder at the summit. He hadn't been experiencing any altitude problems. Could he have made it on his own? Should he have pushed ahead without the others to try, at least?

Dan must have sensed his friend's frustration.

"We'll get it next time, buddy."

But Jared didn't know if there would be a next time. Summer was winding down, and his life in the Air Force was about to begin.

CHAPTER
TWO

Diane McKenney had grown up in Duvall, but she no longer lived there. For the past five years, she'd been living three hundred miles east, in Spokane—first, for undergraduate studies at Gonzaga University, and then graduate school, where she was earning her doctorate in physical therapy at Eastern Washington University.

But she was back in Duvall for the summer, partly to help her mom, who had torn the ACL in her knee and was recovering from surgery. If there was something Diane knew a thing or two about, it was torn ACLs. The anterior cruciate ligament is one of the two ligaments that crisscrosses the knee and allows it to flex the way it's supposed to—and also keeps it from flexing in ways it's *not* supposed to. Tears, especially bad ones, can be seriously debilitating. Without a functioning ACL, it's hard or impossible even to walk: the shinbone keeps trying to slip up in front of the thighbone. Not good.

Diane knew all this even before she started her PT training.

She'd played basketball and volleyball in high school, and loved it. And she was good. She'd hoped to keep playing in college, Division II or III—until she tore the ACL in her own knee, which ended her budding career before it began. She remembered the agony of the injury and the pain of the recovery, and now she had some know-how to be able to make her mom's recovery a little easier.

Diane's ACL injury was a mixed blessing in a way—a case of God closing a door but opening a window. For starters, it forced her out of competitive team sports, and she learned to channel her athletic energies into endurance sports instead. She loved the thrill and discipline of competing with herself. Even now, she was training for her first marathon, and hoped it would be the first of many.

But the other thing the injury had given her was her first exposure to physical therapy—her own—and she discovered she loved it. A lot of what made her a good athlete—her knowledge of the body and how it works, and her commitment and discipline—also made her a good physical therapist. Or anyway, a physical-therapy aide, which is what she would be until she completed her doctorate in two more years.

In a lot of ways, it was good for Diane to be back in Duvall. The years she'd spent living in eastern Washington made her cherish western Washington in new ways, ways she never had while she was growing up. She loved getting to spend some time hiking in the Cascades, and she could see now that people who lived among these mountains didn't always appreciate them; they took them for granted. "Oh, it's raining today; I guess we'll stay inside." She heard people say this all the time. But now, visiting for the summer, she was thoroughly amazed by this terrain that had seemed so normal to her when she was younger: sprawling forests and the majestic Mount Rainier always on the horizon.

Helping her mom was simpler than Diane had imagined it would be. Her mom was athletic and strong-willed—her whole family was—and she was remarkably self-sufficient, even with her injury. But there was one thing that her mom was going to be unable to do, one thing that she wanted Diane to do in her place: summer camp.

Diane's church hosted a summer camp one week each August for its youth group, and Diane had attended the camp once when she was in high school. This year, the camp was on a remote spot of Orcas Island, north of Seattle and right up at the Canadian border. Diane's parents had both volunteered to help out with the camp, but her mom had used up all of her vacation and sick days during her surgery and recovery. She offered Diane her wages for the week so the church didn't have to find another volunteer at the last minute.

Diane didn't exactly relish the idea of going back to her old summer camp as a chaperone; it wasn't how she wanted to close out her summer before going back to Spokane.

But, for her mom—and because she was a financially strapped graduate student—she said yes.

Of course, being back at the camp wound up being fantastic. It was a beautiful environment, full of hiking trails and water activities. Diane's job, mainly, was to enjoy it, to act as a sort of "big sister" and mentor to the high schoolers in camp, and keep them from getting too homesick or getting into trouble. Diane was twenty-three, the perfect age to be able to relate to these teens, while also being able to share some of the wisdom she'd gained since her own high school years.

The week at camp also gave her a chance to get reacquainted with her childhood friend Dan Claussen and his wife, Amber, who were now leading the high school youth group. She'd forgotten how fun Dan could be, and how good he was at organizing adventures.

The two of them were organizing another adventure, it turned out, beginning right after the summer camp wrapped up: they and some friends of theirs were going to climb Mount Rainier. They'd tried it the previous summer, they told her, but they'd had to turn back before they reached the summit. Now they wanted to give it another shot.

"You should come," Dan said to her.

"Really?" Diane asked. She loved hiking, and she was probably in the best shape of her life, but she'd never thought of herself as a mountain climber.

"You're training for a marathon, right? Twenty-six miles? Well, the route we're taking up Rainier is only fifteen miles. It'll be easy."

Diane had known the Claussens long enough not to take their claims of "easy" at face value, but she was also tempted. Mount Rainier! She'd been looking at it, dreaming about it, all summer long, without ever quite imagining that she might have a chance to climb it. What better way to close out the summer before heading back to Spokane? What more exciting way to celebrate all the great feelings she'd been having about western Washington and the Cascades? The mountain!

"I'll think about it," she told him.

And the more she thought about it, the fewer reasons she could come up with not to do it. If it had been Dan's brother, Jon, inviting her, no way! She wouldn't have even considered it. Diane knew Jon Claussen better than she knew Dan, and he was great fun, for sure— but she knew Jon would never choose an "easy" way up Rainier.

Dan, on the other hand, had always seemed calmer and more reasonable. And he'd just married Amber six weeks earlier. No way would he risk starting off their new marriage by getting them killed.

Diane couldn't stop thinking about it. She called an old friend— her first sort-of boyfriend from middle school, who had climbed Rainier as an undergrad and was now one of her good hiking buddies—to ask his opinion.

"Should I do it?" she asked.

To her surprise, he didn't even try to talk her out of it.

"Why *not* do it? You're smart and you're fit; you'll be fine."

Maybe he was right: maybe she would be fine. But Diane thought about her mother, still recovering from her knee surgery. Would her mom be fine? Anyway, they called it "climbing" for a reason. Diane was a hiker, but she wasn't a climber. Climbers had all sorts of gear that Diane knew nothing about—ropes and carabiners and helmets and axes and who knew what else. Even if she could figure out how to use all that gear—which she couldn't!—how would she even get her hands on it? She imagined a shopping trip that would cost hundreds, no, probably thousands of dollars at REI.

But then she remembered her neighbor Mary, a family friend and a very outdoorsy person, who had so much gear in her garage that it might as well *have been* an REI. And Mary was incredibly generous, offering to lend Diane "whatever she needed."

Maybe gear wouldn't be a problem after all.

But was she ready? That was the real question. Was she ready, physically and mentally, to climb the mountain?

How can you even know the answer to that question until you try?

A few days later, on the ferry ride back to Seattle, it was a rare cloudless day, and Mount Rainier was in clear view—like it was taunting her. Dan was listing all the people they knew who had climbed it, hoping to reassure Diane, or maybe peer pressure her.

"If *they* can do it, then you can do it for sure."

But Amber tried a different tactic: "There's a cute guy coming, an Air Force guy who used to work with Dan. His name's Jared. Maybe you two can share a tent."

"Air Force guy?" Diane rolled her eyes. "Not interested." There was an Air Force base in Spokane, and she had seen more than her fill of airmen. That was definitely not something in which she was interested.

What she *was* interested in was climbing Mount Rainier.

"Okay," she told them. "I'll do it."

CHAPTER
THREE

They were already off to a late start, and Jared did his best not to be annoyed. But he *was* annoyed.

It had only been a year and a couple months since he and Dan last tried to summit Rainier, but what a year it had been. Jared felt like a different man.

For starters, he'd spent that year in the military on active duty. He had considered himself a strong, fit person when he'd showed up in Montgomery, Alabama, for the new officer's course, but the rigors of the military took everything to a whole new level. Fitness, he learned, was only partly about the strength of your arms and legs and heart. Just as important, or maybe more important, was the strength of your will. So much of military training in college had been, for Jared, not just about fitness, but also about focus: standing at attention for hours, drilling with bayoneted rifles in the rain, learning to stay cool under all kinds of pressure.

He knew that after his time in Alabama, there was a good chance he would be deployed to Iraq or Afghanistan. Instead, he got assigned to a base in Cheyenne, Wyoming.

As soon as he got there, he started spending every minute of his free time in the mountains.

Most Fridays, as soon as he got off work, he'd climb into his "ultimate *Road Warrior* vehicle"—a thrifty 2009 Hyundai Elantra—and drive to Colorado. He kept the car loaded up with whatever he might need: his tent, sleeping bag, food and water, even an inflatable raft he picked up from Walmart.

Cheyenne, he discovered, was about as flat as Illinois, but also at 6,000 feet of elevation—which meant Jared was already partially acclimated to the thin air when he started climbing Colorado's 14,000-foot peaks each weekend. By the end of that year, he couldn't even count how many "fourteeners" he'd climbed. It was more unusual if a weekend went by *without* him climbing one.

He got better at all of it: the climbing, the rope work, the endurance. He even became inspired by a TV show called *Bear Grylls Survival School* and decided to try spending a night sleeping out in the snow with no tent—just his sleeping bag and whatever protection he could make for himself. He drove up to a mountain and hiked out a little from the trailhead, then used his mountaineering shovel to cut himself a little shelter in the snow, and settled in for a cold night. Well, *half* a night, anyway: after a few hours, he decided to call the experiment a success and spent the rest of the night in the warmth of his car.

Half a night of experience is better than none at all.

But no matter how much he climbed and how hard he trained, it still ate away at him that he hadn't summited Rainier. He wanted to try again, and this time, he wasn't going to let anything stop him.

He called the Claussens and asked if they had any plans to go back to Rainier.

"Ha-ha!" Dan laughed. "Our mom keeps teasing us about turning around last year, so we *have* to go back! It's a point of family pride!"

Jared looked at his schedule and saw he had some vacation time coming at the end of the summer. Some of that was set aside for his sister's wedding in North Carolina, but that still left him almost a week to play with.

A week—plenty of time for a summit trip to Rainier.

Dan wanted to reassemble the crew from the last trip: his wife—Amber—and his old buddy Josh, plus a couple new guys Jared didn't know: Hansen and Mikk. Jared had been working hard all year to become a better climber, but Dan still had a lot more experience than he did—so Jared wanted to defer to Dan on the decision-making.

But he also didn't want anything to get in the way.

"You think they'll be able to make it this time?"

Maybe Dan didn't pick up on the seriousness of Jared's tone, because he just laughed, "You never know with Rainier!"

"I don't want to come all the way out there and not make it to the top, you know?"

Dan had been climbing mountains and vertical rock faces since he was a kid. His family's idea of a vacation was to climb Half Dome together. So he knew that feeling of wanting to summit the mountain.

"Don't worry, man. We'll get you to the top."

But now that Jared was here in Washington, he wasn't so sure. They all should have been on the road by now, but no one seemed to be taking the trip very seriously. He thought they'd all set out around dawn, but everyone decided to go to church in the morning before setting out. And now there was this situation with the backpack.

At the last minute, Dan and Amber had invited an old friend of theirs to join the trip, a cute girl named Diane who, as far as Jared could tell, didn't have any experience at all as a climber or even a backpacker. She was wearing borrowed Gore-Tex pants that didn't quite fit, and while everyone waited, Dan was going through her pack, helping her sort out what she would and wouldn't need.

Jared watched from the distance as Dan went through the girl's toilet kit.

Really? Jared thought to himself. *She brought deodorant? I wonder if there's perfume in there too. Maybe in the bottom of that pack, a pair of stilettos?*

What was she doing on this trip?

Why hadn't they left yet?

He kept his thoughts to himself and pretended to be patient while Dan spread the contents of her pack all over the parking lot. Finally, Jared got tired of waiting.

"Hey," he called out to the group. "I'm gonna head over to that bookstore. Grab me whenever you're ready."

There was nothing he wanted from the bookstore, of course. What he wanted was to be climbing up the mountain. But as he wandered through the stacks of books to distract himself from his frustration, he found a book on World War II that he found intriguing, so he bought it. By the time he got back to the parking lot, they were just finishing loading up the two cars.

The drive from Duvall to the Paradise trailhead takes a little over three hours on a good day. But it didn't turn out to be a good day. The Claussens took unusual pride in driving ancient and dilapidated cars into the ground, and the old-model Corolla that Dan and Amber were driving was in no shape for the climb to Paradise, at 5,420 feet. The car putt-putted up the switchbacks, sometimes so slowly that

Jared wondered if it would help for him to get out and push. They had to pull the car over because of overheating, pop the hood to let out the steam, and then pour water into the radiator to replace what had evaporated. And then, a few miles later, they had to do it again. And again.

And because the trip was taking so long, everyone was getting hungry, so before they got to the park, they decided to stop for pizza.

"Let's get it to go," Jared suggested.

But the group decided it would be nice to have a sit-down dinner.

At this rate, they'd be lucky to get to Paradise by sunset.

By the time they left the pizza place, the Corolla's engine had cooled off, at least, and they got through the rest of the drive without incident. They crossed into the national park and arrived at the Paradise Ranger Station—as Jared had guessed—right around sunset.

Their two cars paused in front of the sign that posted the park's fees. In addition to the national park admission fee, there was also a "Climbing Cost Recovery Fee" that was an additional thirty dollars per climber. Climbers were supposed to put their fee inside an envelope with their contact information and leave it in a lockbox. Dan was furious.

"Are you kidding me? Thirty dollars each? That's not right. These are God's mountains."

The group needed to decide: they could all camp out here in Paradise and start the first part of the climb in the morning, or they could leave immediately for the first leg of the hike and then sleep in the hut at Camp Muir. Either choice had its advantage: Everyone was a little tired from the long drive, and it might be nice to call it an early night and then start tomorrow totally refreshed. But if they muscled through and hiked tonight, that would be a quick 4,660 feet they could put behind them, and it would give them an entire day at Camp Muir, a chance to acclimate to the 10,080-foot air before pushing the rest of the way to the summit.

Dan didn't have a strong preference, and while the rest of the team debated the options, he focused his attention on shooing away a pesky fox that kept trying to raid their packs.

"Get out of here!"

The fox gave him a savvy look, like it had seen way too many tourists, and kept moving toward their packs. Dan scoured the parking lot, looking for a stone or a pinecone, anything he could throw to scare off the fox, but he couldn't find anything. He reached into his pocket and grabbed something—a piece of chocolate—and tossed it. It skittered across the pavement, and the fox grabbed it and ran.

"Hey!" a voice called out from the darkness as a park ranger stepped out of the shadows toward Dan.

"I'm gonna have to write you up for that. No feeding the animals."

". . . the most luxuriant and the most extravagantly beautiful of all the alpine gardens I ever beheld in all my mountain-top wanderings."

—John Muir, conservationist, 1889

Group photo at dusk leaving from Paradise on the Skyline Trail, headed for Camp Muir, August 29, 2010. Left to Right: Amber Claussen, Dan Claussen, Hansen Topp, Josh Bresler, Jared Rund, Mikk Kaschko, and Diane McKenney.

"What?"

"There's no feeding the animals," the ranger repeated.

"Feeding the—? I wasn't feeding him, I was trying to—!!"

The ranger didn't want to hear it. He was already lecturing about the balance of the park's ecosystem while writing out a $125 citation. He tore off the crinkly yellow copy and handed it to Dan.

"Don't do it again."

"I didn't do it *this* time!"

But the ranger was already

gone, leaving Dan staring after him in annoyed frustration, and everyone else trying to understand what had just happened.

"Well, that settles it," Dan said to the group. "No way am I staying here tonight. And no way am I paying that thirty-dollar climbing fee, either! Let's go."

CHAPTER
FOUR

AUGUST 29, 2010

9:00 P.M.

Diane felt good. It had been a long day and she knew she should be tired, but she wasn't. She felt energized, and the crisp night air made her feel even better.

The group climbed the stone steps out of the Paradise parking lot single file, each of them wearing a headlamp to light their way through the dark. The trail was immediately steep, even the paved part, but leveled off a bit once it switched to dirt. A whole maze of trails crisscrossed these meadows, but Dan led the way and the others followed until they arrived at the path that would take them up the mountain: the Skyline Trail.

The Skyline Trail is famous for its view of avalanche lilies and other wildflowers that stretched colorfully throughout the valleys at Rainier's base—not that Diane could see any of that in the dark. The view she had consisted of whatever she could see in the light of her headlamp.

The group walked through tall pine trees and over an area where an avalanche had cluttered the path a bit with rocks, and then began a series of steep switchbacks. As they climbed, the trees thinned and the view opened up at a spot called Panorama Point, though Diane didn't see much of a panorama in the darkness.

The trail was getting steeper now, but she still didn't feel tired. If this was as hard as Rainier was going to be, she'd be fine. Her rented mountaineering boots felt stiff, different from her usual hiking boots, and she hadn't gotten used to them yet. They squeaked when she walked, and now that the steep trail had cut down on the group's chatter, the squeaking of her boots was all she could hear, over and over and over; she couldn't stop hearing it. She was glad to be here, and smiled. That Air Force guy, Jared, saw her smiling, and he smiled too.

She didn't know what to make of Jared. He was quiet and maybe a little arrogant, she thought. She'd noticed him watching while Dan was repacking her bag; she'd felt him judging her.

Whatever he was thinking about her, she wanted to prove him wrong. What was it with Air Force guys and their unflappable self-confidence? Was that what they taught in the Air Force: that you are always right and everyone else is probably wrong?

He must have known she was thinking about him, because suddenly he spoke to her.

"I was up here last year with Dan, and we were here during the daylight. On a clear day, you can see down to Mount Hood in Oregon."

I know where Mount Hood is, she thought.

But she saw that he was being sweet, or trying, anyway. Maybe she was wrong about him. Maybe he was nervous or excited about the climb. Maybe he was kind of shy.

One thing was certain: he sure seemed happy to be on the mountain. And, like her, he didn't seem to be having any trouble with the climb. The two of them walked close together in long, easy strides.

The path was covered in snow that had been packed down by lots of previous footsteps, and it was easy to stay on the path: it was the only one, and it went up. Behind them, Josh was bringing up the rear, already feeling the altitude and the pizza he knew he shouldn't have had earlier, huffing and puffing and struggling to keep up. Josh was a few years older than Diane and they'd known each other since they were kids. He'd always acted a little protective, like a big brother. *Well, if he wants to be protective*, she thought, *he'd better keep up!*

"Come on, Josh. You've got this!"

Diane knew this climb meant a lot to him. He'd been part of the failed summit attempt last year, and since then, he'd been eating a lot healthier and running. And he'd grown up listening to stories of his own father's summit of the mountain—an expedition on which his dad had broken a leg and climbed on it most of the way down before finally getting help from the rangers.

Josh gave her a weary thumbs-up but didn't spend any breath trying to answer.

Jared gave Josh an encouraging pat on the back, and it seemed to boost Josh's spirits a little.

Maybe I was wrong about this guy, she thought again.

Soon they were above the trees and crossing the Muir Snowfield. It was strange. There are no trails on Rainier above 8,000 feet or so—because at that elevation, there's no dirt or vegetation or anything to make a trail *through* or make a trail *with*. Above 8,000 feet, Rainier is nothing but volcanic rock, snow, and ice. The paths are marked by the mountain guides and rangers, who plant little flags in the ground to help guide hikers through the otherwise hard-to-distinguish terrain.

Diane didn't think much about it though. Dan and the others

knew where they were going, and all she had to do was follow along. But the snowfield seemed endless, and who knew how long they had been hiking in the dark—four hours? Six? She was exhausted. They all were. Her mind dropped into a sort of trance state, the same way it did when she was running: she put one foot in front of the other and didn't think at all, about anything, and in that trance, she felt like she could probably go on like this forever.

Finally, she heard a cheer from the front of the line, and she knew even before she saw it that they were there, at Camp Muir. One final, steep push, and they'd made it.

Camp Muir sits in the middle of the Muir Snowfield at 10,080 feet, one last stopping point before seven different paths up to the summit. It's a small complex of buildings: a ranger station—a stone shack, really—and an A-frame hut that hosts a few professional mountain guides who lead paying tourists to the summit. But the centerpiece of the camp, and the one the hikers were most excited to see, was the old stone structure where they'd be sleeping. Built in 1921, the hut doesn't have any amenities—but it's got four walls that keep out the wind, or most of it, and bunks for two dozen people.

The camp was named for the Scottish-American naturalist John Muir, who summited Rainier in 1888 and who is one of the main people responsible for getting the mountain designated a national park in 1899. In fact, it's fair to say that Muir is a big part of why the United States has national parks at all: he championed the creation of Yosemite and Sequoia National Parks, helped found the Sierra Club, and is the namesake for numerous camps, colleges, monuments, and trails, including a 210-mile trail that runs through most of California's Sierra Nevadas.

Almost everyone who is dedicated enough to make it as far up

Mount Rainier as Camp Muir is likely familiar with the man who shares its name, and likely grateful to him for the work he did to preserve America's wildlands. Climbers coming into this camp for the first time can't help but feel like they're a part of something historic and wonderful.

But they're grateful, too, for the bunks.

When Diane and the others arrived at Camp Muir, it was mostly empty. Climbers aiming for Rainier's summit generally depart between 11:00 p.m. and midnight, and that meant they were already gone. Other than a few guided tour groups, they had the place to themselves—and they had nearly twenty-four hours here at Camp Muir before they'd be setting out again.

What they wanted now was sleep.

When Diane awoke the next morning, she couldn't remember immediately where she was. Then it came to her: *I'm on the mountain!* She peered out through a crack in the stone hut and saw the ice-blue sky and felt the chilly wind. It was amazing.

After getting out of bed, she saw Dan and Jared talking to one of the rangers.

"What's up?" she asked them when they were done. "What were you all talking about?"

"The only thing anyone ever talks about this far up on Rainier," Dan answered, "is the weather. The ranger told us it's quite windy, but it's clear."

The Pacific Northwest is already notorious for its heavy rains, but Rainier is something else altogether. The mountain is so high and its ice, so massive, that it literally makes its own weather. It blocks off the fronts from the ocean, cools the warm sea air, and creates a meteorologist's nightmare. Clear skies give way to blinding snowstorms with almost no warning.

The ranger told them that over the next day there was a pretty high probability of gusting winds, and a small chance of snow.

Dan looked up at the sky, which was clear as could be.

"Yeah, okay. Unless something changes, let's stick to the plan."

While the others were melting snow to fill their water bottles—the only source of water this high up on the mountain—Dan was teaching Diane some fundamentals of mountaineering and glacier travel.

"These big spiky things are called crampons."

Diane could feel Jared watching again.

"I know what crampons are, Dan!"

"Okay, good—but have you ever worn them?"

She had to admit she hadn't.

"Stomp around a little; get used to them. You're taller now, and you're spiky, so if you're not careful, you can hurt people. If you drag your feet, you will plant your face in the snow; I guarantee it."

"Hey! Didn't you promise me climbing Rainier would be just like running?"

Dan considered this.

"It is just like running—with big spiky crampons on your feet. Now let's try the ice axe!"

By the end of the afternoon, Diane was—well, she wouldn't call herself an expert, by any means—but she was feeling completely competent. The thing they worked on most was "self-arresting": using your ice axe to stop you from sliding off the mountain.

"You can see why that's important, right?" Dan asked.

And she agreed; she did not want to slide off the mountain. So even when Dan was confident that she had it figured out, she practiced a little bit longer.

While she and Dan were working on this, everyone else tried to relax. Jared dug a few holes in the dirt and gathered up some rocks to teach the others how to play an old strategy game called mancala. They took turns "sowing" and doing "relays" and capturing each other's pieces until the game was over.

The weather remained clear, for now, and everyone gave more and more thought to the summit. They would set their alarms for 11:30 p.m., and that meant they'd want to call it an early night and get to bed by 6:00 or 6:30 p.m. They ate an early dinner, and Josh told the group he wasn't planning to go ahead with the climb. He cited the pizza and the altitude, saying he wasn't feeling well enough and didn't want to slow anyone down.

Josh staying behind was demoralizing, but he also offered them a huge favor that would increase their own odds of summiting. Since he'd be staying at Camp Muir, it gave the others a chance to leave unnecessary gear behind, cut some pack weight, and carry only the barest essentials to the summit. Every ounce they could remove from their packs would help save them from fatigue on their climb, so they began sorting through their gear, making decisions about what they did and didn't need. All of them were grateful to free up the weight of their cell phones, camp stoves, and the extra food they'd brought in case they wound up having to spend some extra time at base camp. But their plan now was for a vigorous overnight push to the top, then down again to Camp Muir before a late lunch the following day. No one wanted to sleep on the cold, windy mountaintop, so there was no need for anyone to bring tents, stoves, or sleeping bags to the summit.

"Well, maybe we should bring one or two sleeping bags," Dan suggested, "in case anyone wants to warm up during one of our breaks." Jared had an ultralight down sleeping bag that added almost no weight to his pack, so he agreed to carry his for the trip.

After dinner, Diane stretched out on her bunk and thought about the summit. It was still miles away, and they were hard miles. There were still 4,000 feet of elevation to climb, in ever-thinning air, across glaciers. Until today, Diane had never set foot on a glacier. But later tonight she would be making her way to the top of Mount Rainier. It was hard for her to guess what this would even be like, what her next day would hold—and not knowing filled her with excitement and also a little fear.

She looked at Jared next to her on the bunk. He wasn't sleeping either. How could any of them sleep with this adventure only a few hours away?

Just as she thought this, Josh's loud snoring cut through the quiet of the cabin, and she and Jared laughed out loud. Of course Josh could sleep. He didn't have a mountain to climb!

She and Jared shook their heads and smiled at each other again, and then they stared at the ceiling, waiting for the time to tick by.

CHAPTER
FIVE

AUGUST 31, 2010

2:00 A.M.

Jared was happy with the pace Dan set up the mountain—not so fast that it would tire people out, but also quick enough that they hoped they could all make it to the top and back before the weather turned.

There was still no guessing the weather: it was the dead of night and skies were ink black because of clouds high overhead. Would they blow over and clear? Would they dump hail and sleet and snow? It was impossible to say. All they could do was keep climbing and hope for the best.

The group followed the ranger-marked route of bamboo sticks with orange flags to the top of the Muir Snowfield, and then crossed onto the Cowlitz Glacier, the first of three distinct glaciers they would have to traverse to make it to the summit.

It's hard to fully understand a glacier until you're standing on one. At its simplest, a glacier is a sheet of ice—very thick, very old ice. But that doesn't begin to describe the enormity—the *experience*—of a glacier.

A glacier forms wherever the yearly snowfall is greater than the yearly snowmelt. Snow piles up and freezes year after year, higher and higher, deeper and deeper. This goes on for years or even centuries, and as time passes, this freeze gets more and more massive, reaching a thickness that's sometimes a hundred feet, and occasionally, almost a mile.

As this ice accumulates, it also grows in weight, and the weight begins to change it: it pushes down, compressing itself and making the deeper ice denser. Glacier ice gets so dense that it's able to absorb all but the bluest of light—which is why it often looks blue. As this giant mass of ice weighs down on itself, it pushes down on the ground beneath it too, crumbling all but the strongest rock. The downward pressure of all this ice also generates, ironically, heat. The pressure from the top of the glacier forces the deepest parts of the glacier to melt.

This cycle—snow piling on top, freezing and adding more pressure and causing melting on the bottom—means a glacier is always shifting. It grows and shrinks. It cracks and pops and moves and almost breathes. This is what you don't fully understand until you're standing on top of one, hearing the glacier breathing beneath you: it is practically a living thing. And like so many living things, a glacier can have bad moods.

As it melts and shifts, this giant sheet of ice laid across the landscape inevitably cracks, and whenever it does, each crack can be gigantic, opening up a deep, seemingly bottomless chasm called a "crevasse." A small crevasse might be thirty feet long and a few feet across, but the biggest ones are monstrous: fifty feet across or more, half a mile long, and hundreds of feet deep—plenty deep enough to swallow climbers.

As if that weren't harrowing enough, every snowstorm has the potential to cover the tops of the crevasses with a layer of snow, rendering them invisible. When the snow is thick enough, this can be a boon for a climber, because it may create a "snow bridge" that safely spans the width of the crevasse. But if the snow *isn't* thick enough, then the snow bridge can collapse into the crevasse without warning: a climber's nightmare.

Anyone who hopes to cross a glacier—so, everyone who attempts to reach the summit of Mount Rainier—will encounter crevasses, hundreds of them. The path to the top requires charting a path around them or, in some cases, across them.

The orange flags that rangers and professional guides use to mark the trail are meant to offer climbers a zigzag route around the known and most treacherous crevasses. But a glacier is a living organism, and conditions are always changing on the mountain. Old crevasses can close and new ones can open, and this cycle is made worse in the warm summer months, when the glaciers are melting and cracking. One reason climbers aim for Rainier's summit at night is that it's safest to cross the glaciers during the coldest hours of night, rather than during daylight, when the sun weakens the snow bridges, melts icy overhangs, and opens up new crevasses without warning.

Dan's job as the team leader was to follow the course the rangers had set out, and also to understand the conditions of the ice well enough that he could improvise when needed.

Jared's job, as he saw it, was not to fall in.

Last year's trip to Rainier had been his first experience with glacier travel and an occasional scramble up more vertical ice, using the sharp metal crampons on his boots to dig his feet into the dense ice for traction and swinging his ice axe into the glacier to gain leverage on the steep climbs. He'd come to love his ice axe. It not only made difficult climbs possible, but it was also a potential lifesaver: If you start sliding down the side of an icy mountain, your hands won't be able to stop your fall. Only the teeth of the axe's pick or the sharp spike at the tip of its handle will be able to keep you from plunging off the mountain. Even on the gentler parts of the climb, the ice axe came in handy, doubling as a hiking pole for extra leverage and offering a relatively safe way to poke at a snow bridge to test its strength.

Somewhere along the way, the snow had started falling. This was not uncommon this late in the climbing season. It wasn't terrible—not yet—but it was a grim reminder that things might get worse for them. It also made everything harder to see. In the dark, their headlamps could shine fifty feet ahead, but the snowfall had begun to cut that distance in half. He could see what was in front of him, but he couldn't always see Dan at the head of the group.

Oh well, he thought. *I guess I'm not here for the view.*

Even in the dark, Jared could see the terrain around them changing. Not long after leaving Camp Muir, and for the first time, the team decided to "rope up": tether to a partner so that one person could help provide leverage for another, and help catch them if they were to slip.

Because Jared was closest to her on the trail, he roped up with the girl.

He didn't mind doing it. Though he'd originally imagined her as some frivolous flake, a "Backpacking Barbie," she seemed to be handling herself well on the climb. She was in good spirits and in good shape, and she had a fun sense of humor too. She didn't have any experience on the ice at all, and this worried him a little—but he hadn't had any experience either, last year, on his first trip up this mountain. He decided that if he could, he'd try to help her get to the top.

"Here," he said, tying the two of them together from his harness. "You go first, and I'll keep an eye on you."

She smiled at him.

"Thanks."

He watched as she climbed on, strong and athletic.

I wish I could remember her name, Jared thought.

For the most part, they'd been weaving a path around the crevasses past Camp Muir, but before long, they came to a smallish one and the route had them go right over it. The crevasse was only a couple feet, and on dry land, none of them would have thought much of doing it—but up here in the snow, wearing backpacks and heavy boots with spikes, even a small step or jump seemed challenging.

One by one, they lined up at the lip of the crevasse, and made their way over it.

Last year, when he'd done this for the first time, Jared remembered it feeling momentous. This time, he was surprised by how easy it seemed to him, how routine. He smiled at the realization: He was a mountaineer now. This was what he did—for fun.

They made their way over Cathedral Gap and onto the Ingraham Glacier, the one they planned to follow nearly to the top of the mountain.

Shortly after passing the Ingraham Flats camp, the team came to another crevasse. This one was far too wide to jump across. Instead, there was an aluminum ladder secured to the ice and straddling the crevasse. A plank had been laid down on top of the rungs of the ladder, making the walk across straightforward, as long as you didn't think too much about what you were doing: walking on a ladder across a chasm in the ice!

Jared was no fan of these ladder crossings—but at least this ladder had planks. Last year, he'd had to cross one of these while walking on the metal rungs, in crampons. That was harrowing. Compared to that, this was, well, walking the plank. He didn't overthink it. He didn't look down. He walked the plank—and wound up on the other side.

Up to their right was a jagged set of rocks called Disappointment Cleaver that jutted out above the glaciated ice like a mountainous row of teeth. It is surrounded by glaciers on both sides and is one of the only recognizable landmarks—one of the most visible bits of something other than ice—on the climb to the top. As morbid as its name sounds, a "cleaver" is just the term for any rocky junction that divides two glaciers. As for the "Disappointment" part of its name, no one knows for sure where that comes from, but Jared certainly had a guess: he remembered seeing Disappointment Cleaver on his last climb, when he was feeling a great deal of disappointment about having been forced to turn around. He wondered how many climbers over the years had endured that same experience—to get this far up the mountain only to call it quits.

Not this year, he thought, determined.

Some of the paths to the summit led around the cleaver and climbed up on its far side. It might seem, given the choice between climbing the glacier and all its crevasses or climbing rock, that the rock would be a welcome relief—but in reality, the opposite is true. The brittle volcanic rock is not only hard to climb, but also dangerous: it's prone to breaking, slipping out from under your feet, or, worse, falling from somewhere far overhead. Some very skilled climbers have died from avalanches at Disappointment Cleaver, but it doesn't take a whole avalanche to kill a person. Being in the path of one falling rock or chunk of ice is just as deadly.

The group had planned to climb directly up the 30-degree-steep Ingraham Glacier, a short, direct route. But this path offered dangers: its crevasses were opening wider and more frequently during these warmest summer months, and it was also laced with seracs—high columns of ice that could crack loose and plummet down in giant blocks, sweeping out everything in their path before smashing thousands of feet below.

But when they came to the Ingraham Glacier, they saw their "direct route" was nothing of the sort. Its ice was ripped up by exposed crevasses. It would be almost impossible to cross safely.

Their only good choice was to climb Disappointment Cleaver. At a few points during the climb, Jared looked over his shoulder, hoping for a glimpse of the outline of the sharp, picturesque peak of Little Tahoma, a mini summit off to their right. He remembered it from last year's climb. He recalled that it had been the last major landmark they'd seen before they decided to turn around. He wanted to see it so he could be sure they had put it behind them. But today, in the early hours before dawn, all he could see was clouds and darkness. The team continued its slow but steady climb on up the cleaver, carefully placing every step on the loose rock and listening for any sign of rock falling from above.

After another hour or so, he saw the front of his group was at a standstill. He caught up to them as quickly as he could to see why they were stopped.

Since the group had been climbing single file or in pairs the whole way, this was the first time in a while Jared had seen Dan and Amber. Even now, up close, it was hard to get a bead on them; their faces were bundled up against the cold and obscured as a result of the low visibility.

"What's going on?" Jared shouted over the wind. He had a

sinking feeling, the worst sort of déjà vu.

Dan called back to him, "Amber and I are gonna turn around. She doesn't like this wind."

Amber looked worried. The never-ending powerful gusts of wind were getting to her. She didn't feel comfortable on the ice and snow around all the crevasses in these conditions. She also saw the headlamps of a group below them shifting their path down the mountain. Was one of the guided groups turning around already? Or was it another group the team had not seen at Camp Muir before they embarked on their summit push?

"We are gonna head back to Muir," Dan said. "But I think the rest of you should keep going."

"Yeah?" Jared asked.

"Sure. You and Mikk have experience up here. You've got this. Get up there and take a pretty picture for us when you reach the top."

They spent another minute talking to the girl, Backpacker Barbie, whatever her name was. She was only on this trip because of them, and Dan had promised to see her safely to the summit and back. Now it seemed like they were trying to decide whether or not she should keep going. Jared couldn't hear what they were saying, but the gist of it was clear: she did not want to turn around.

Dan pulled an extra down jacket out of his pack and gave it to Jared to carry, then turned to the rest of the group.

"Guys!" he called out. "You keep an eye on her!" He checked his watch. "It's 4:00 a.m. right now. Follow the flags, and you'll hit the summit in a few hours. We'll see you back at Camp Muir around 1:00 p.m."

And with that, Dan went down the mountain with his wife, and the rest of the team kept climbing up.

CHAPTER
SIX

AUGUST 31, 2010

5:30 A.M.

Diane had never climbed Mount Rainier before, so she didn't have any baseline to measure whether or not this was "normal," but she didn't need any particular experience to know that the weather on the mountain was definitely not good. The wind gusts were the strongest she had ever experienced, and what had started as a gentle snow had grown more insistent, and then turned into high-velocity pellets of ice. They trudged up the mountain mostly with their eyes closed, squinting against the hail at each orange flag to try and spot the next one up the mountain.

It had been maybe ninety minutes since Dan and Amber had turned around and there was still no sign of the summit. As long as they kept following the flags, it was impossible to get lost—at least in theory—but rangers and guides would add new flags as the crevasses opened later in the climbing season, charting a new, safer course. But that meant every once in a while, they would find competing—and confusing—flags.

Up. No matter what, they knew the summit was up.

But there were a few troubles with "up." The weather was getting worse and there was no shelter from the wind; in fact, the wind all seemed to be funneling up and around the mountain, bouncing back at them, blowing from every direction.

Also, the higher they got, the thinner the air grew. Hansen was throwing up. At first, he tried blaming it on the Goldschläger shots he and a few other team members had shared the night before to celebrate the adventure. But as time went by, the truth was obvious enough: he was showing all the signs of Acute Mountain Sickness, and it wasn't getting any better.

"You see that?" Jared asked.

The wind had died down for a merciful few moments, and in the calm, they could see, down the glacier, a group of climbers.

"Must be one of those guided tours," Jared said.

"Yeah," Mikk agreed. "And they're heading down, not up."

"Back from the summit, you think?"

"No way. They started after us, and they're below us now. They must've called it quits."

They watched as the guided group receded in the distance.

"You know what?" Hansen said. "I'm gonna join them. I feel terrible, and this is as good a chance as I'm gonna get to hitch a ride back to Camp Muir." Before anyone had time to argue, he set off down the glacier, racing to catch up with the descending group.

Mikk looked at Jared and Diane. It was just the three of them now.

"What do you think?" he asked. "Should we join him? Should we head down?"

Jared looked at his watch and then at the murky sky.

"You should if you want to. But we're almost there. I'm going to keep going."

Diane agreed, "No point going this far and quitting."

Mikk nodded, and the three of them started climbing back up the trail.

Diane preparing to cross a ladder with wooden planks and a safety rope fixed by Rainier mountain guides.

Diane lost a glove. She wasn't even sure how it happened. The leash of her ice axe must have gotten tangled up in the glove and yanked it loose when she was trying to get some water from her bottle, and then a gust of wind must have carried it clear off her hand. Now it was forty feet below them, across a sheet of ice and snow that was probably forty-five degrees steep.

"Uh—guys?" she called out.

They all agreed she shouldn't try to do the rest of the climb without the glove. It was too cold, especially with all this wind. But none of them saw an easy way to get to where the glove was now resting.

"What are we gonna do?" Mikk asked. He was already exhausted. Any uncharted snow and ice on the glacier might hide a crevasse underneath it. The prospect of climbing forty feet down presented a high risk for a potentially fatal fall.

But she was going to need that glove.

Jared looked around and thought about the gear he had in his pack.

"I think I can get it," he said to Mikk, "if you can belay me."

"Belaying" was one of the things Dan had shown to Diane during her crash course in climbing at Camp Muir the day before. "But don't worry," he'd told her. "You won't actually need to do any of this."

The principle of it was simple enough: one climber anchors a rope and keeps it under tension, and the other climber, attached to the rope, goes up or down. As long as it's done right, belaying should keep a climber from ever falling any farther than the amount of slack that's on the rope. This allows climbers to take risks that would be too dangerous without a belay.

That's all good in theory. It's slightly more involved when you're on a sheet of ice with forty-mile-per-hour winds gusting.

Jared and Mikk assayed the area to try to find the best place for Mikk to anchor and for Jared to climb down. Diane, out of her element, didn't know how to help and did her best to stay out of their way.

When it was all set up, Jared called out, "Ready to climb!"

"Belay ready," Mikk answered.

Slowly, carefully, Jared made his way down. He inched down the ice until he'd used up the slack on the rope, dug in his crampons and axe, and waited while Mikk fed out a little more slack, just enough for Jared to be able to make the next step. They worked like this, in tandem, step by step, lowering Jared nearly to the full length of his climbing rope. He was still a long reach from the glove.

He realized that if he reached for it and missed, he might knock it the rest of the way down the mountain—and all this effort would have been for nothing. He took a deep breath, reached, and grabbed it.

Diane let out a little cheer. Then the guys repeated their process in reverse, Jared climbing up, faster now, while Mikk worked to keep the rope under tension in case Jared lost his footing.

At the end of the endeavor, Diane was reunited with her glove—but they'd lost half an hour. Whatever energy Mikk had left was nearly spent.

"Let's get to the top already," he said, though the look on his face said he wasn't all that sure he'd make it.

Diane's watch read 7:00 a.m. They should have been there by now—and they all knew it. The weather had gone from bad to worse, and every step up the mountain was excruciatingly slow. Mountains get harder to climb the higher they go. The easy dirt paths at the bottom gradually give way to rock, snow, and ice. The trees, which provide shelter from the wind and sun at lower elevations, thin out and eventually vanish at higher elevations. The temperature drops. The route gets steeper. Fatigue sets in; imagine being on a StairMaster for seven hours!

But, to make things worse, the air gets thinner—exponentially thinner—with every upward step. Work that felt easy at 5,000 feet feels hard at 10,000 feet, and harder at 11,000, and harder still at 12,000, 13,000, wherever they were now.

Walking in crampons up a 30-degree sheet of ice isn't "walking" at all. It requires kicking one spiky foot hard into the ice, testing its leverage, and inching upward, then digging the spike or pick of the ice axe in to provide some upper-body support, then yanking the other foot out of its anchor in the ice and kicking it in another step up—over and over and over. It was exhausting.

During one of their now-frequent rests, the three of them looked below them and saw, in the distance, a crowd of climbers roped together, heading down the mountain.

"Looks like that other guided group decided to turn around," Diane said.

"Smart group," Mikk said. The fatigue was wearing all of them down. "Guys, all of my water is frozen. I think I'm gonna wait here for you guys to bag the summit, then we can hike down together."

Jared nodded somberly. Then he turned to look at Diane.

"What?" she asked.

"I'm thinking maybe you should wait here too."

In that moment, the wind blasted them and cut off the conversation. She wasn't sure she'd heard him right. Was he telling her to stay with Mikk? After coming all this way?

"Why would I do that?" she demanded.

"Look," Jared said. "I've never been up here. I don't know how far the summit is. And the weather is definitely getting worse. If you go with me, I can't guess how long it'll take to reach the summit. I can't promise I can keep you safe."

He didn't think she could do it, even after everything they'd been through. But also this guy, this Air Force guy, he was going to keep charging up the mountain no matter what. He had just admitted he was planning to charge straight into a snowstorm even though he didn't know where he was going or how long it would take. If she climbed down the mountain with Mikk, then Jared would be up here alone, left to his own stubborn decision-making. He might get himself killed.

"Well," she answered, "I can't promise I can keep you safe either!"

They filled up Mikk's water bottle with the water they had left and continued up the mountain. The two of them still had a two waters bottles left, but the water inside of these bottles was frozen solid.

"It's okay," Jared said. "We'll keep them inside our coats so they'll thaw out."

They moved the icy water bottles into their down jackets and looked up to where they knew the crest of the mountain must be.

"Let's do it," Diane said, and led the climb toward the crater rim.

She hoped she'd made the right decision.

CHAPTER
SEVEN

AUGUST 31, 2010

7:45 A.M.

Jared was starting to wonder if he'd made the right decision. Almost an hour had passed since they'd parted ways with Mikk, and they still weren't at the summit. They absolutely should have been there by now, but the visibility was so bad that he couldn't see the top of the mountain, couldn't even guess where the top of the mountain was. The snow and clouds had increased to the point that he and the girl could barely see each other.

They had come upon another ladder, ascending steeply across a wide crevasse. The last ladder they had crossed had planks laid across it and a safety rope running alongside, so each climber could clip him- or herself in to protect against an unlucky fall. But this new ladder was just a ladder—no planks, only bare rungs and a more vertical pitch. It was anchored to the ground and tied down, and Jared tested the ladder's stability.

"Seems okay," he said, though neither one of them were especially eager to climb the thing. The metal crampons against the ladder rungs were awkward and even a little slippery, and he wondered if they'd be better taking them off for this part of the climb.

But he was also worried about time, so he put his concerns aside and stepped onto the ladder, taking it step by step, trying not to notice the way the aluminum bent and bounced when he was in the middle of the crevasse. And getting off the ladder and back onto the ice was harrowing too. He wound up using his ice axe for a little extra leverage.

Once he was standing on the far side, he called back, "Okay, it's all good. Take it slow. And try not to look down!"

He waited by the ledge while she slowly shinnied up, trying not to think too much about the passing time. They had made a deal with each other: they would turn around at 8:00 a.m., whether they'd made it to the top or not. It was a smart, if heartbreaking, thing for him to concede. They should have summited more than an hour ago, and instead, they were still trudging slowly up this seemingly endless mountain, with no end in sight. Meanwhile, their friends were waiting for them back at Camp Muir and would be expecting everyone to reconvene in a few more hours for the trek back off the mountain.

Jared knew it would be unwise to get caught on the glacier during daylight, at least as much as they could avoid it. All the dangers the glacier presented were made worse by the sun. Though the sunlight wouldn't feel especially warm to a climber, it was warm enough to affect the ice: during the day, crevasses would shift and open, snow bridges would get thinner, and melting snow could cause deadly avalanches. Turning around by 8:00 a.m. would put them on schedule to be safely off the glacier and back at Camp Muir before the warmest part of day.

But, of course, they didn't want to turn around. They wanted to find their way to the top. It was crazy-making, knowing they must be so close to the summit without actually being able to find it in all this blinding snow.

If only I had a GPS, Jared thought for the hundredth time.

He did own a GPS device—a lightweight and not-inexpensive wrist-worn Garmin Foretrex that was great at pinpointing his exact location on a map, even when he was out of cell range. He'd been using it all year on his mountain adventures in Colorado, and it had helped him out on more than one occasion when the mountain paths had disoriented him. It would have been perfect here, too, to guide them the rest of the way up Rainier. But now that he needed it, where was that GPS device? It was in Colorado, in the back of his buddy Gavin's SUV, where he'd left it last weekend. He laughed at the stupidity of it. It had never occurred to him to bring it with him to Washington; he'd never thought he would need it. He knew he'd be climbing with Dan and a half-dozen other people, most of whom had their own GPS devices, and they'd be going up a route that was traveled by thousands of other people every summer. What were the odds of getting lost?

Not zero, it turned out.

"Hey," the girl said. She pointed up ahead to a lip of icy rock. "Is that the rim?" she asked.

Mount Rainier is a giant cone-shaped "stratovolcano," and the top of the mountain—the tip of the cone—is a broad valley made up of two overlapping volcanic craters. A climber aiming for the summit first has to make his or her way up the steep outer rim of these craters, and then step down into the circular volcanic valley that makes up the top of the mountain. You know you're close to the summit when you cross this rim.

"I think that is the rim!" Jared answered.

They both found a new reserve of energy and sped up their climb toward this, even though it was very steep. Jared reached the rim first and poked his head over it to look down into Rainier's cone—and as soon as he did, he got clipped by a blast of wind so strong it nearly knocked him backward down the mountain. The wind had been intense for hours, but here at the top, there was nothing to block or buffer it, no shelter at all, and the force of it was literally breathtaking.

"Whoa!" he said out loud. Then, "Watch your step," as he offered her a hand over the crest of the crater.

They climbed over the rim and down into the crater. They were standing inside one of the biggest, most dangerous volcanoes in the world, and though it hadn't erupted in over a hundred years, it would still rumble to remind people that it wasn't fully asleep, either. This round valley at the top of the mountain was a caldera—a sunken area left from an old eruption. It stretched maybe a quarter mile across and had two overlapping craters down in its center, belching a sulfur smell from deep inside the earth.

But they weren't at the top yet.

The rim stretched skyward into three distinct peaks, each one with its own name: the Liberty Cap, which measured 14,112 feet; Point Success, 14,158 feet; and the highest one, their final destination, Columbia Crest, which was 14,411 feet.

They trekked the final distance across the crater toward the Columbia Crest. Only 261 feet of elevation gain, Jared remembered reading, from the rim to the summit—less than a football field—but the spiteful wind that was raging made them earn every single step.

Finally, they got there: the top of Mount Rainier, the tallest mountain in the Pacific Northwest, the fifth tallest in the continental United States. After a few intense minutes of searching through the fresh snow, they found the shiny metal "U.S. Geological Survey

Benchmark" that had been hammered into the surveyed highest point.

"I want to get a picture," Jared said as they stood by the marker, and he started digging through his pack for the little camera he'd brought for this occasion. He knew that on a clear day, the view from the top of Rainier was supposed to be extraordinary. It was an observation deck that showcased Seattle, the Pacific Ocean, Mount Adams, Mount Saint Helens, Mount Hood, Mount Jefferson, and some days, even Mount Shasta, even Canada.

Today, though, he could barely see his hand in front of his face. They'd have to settle for a selfie next to the geomarker. But the camera wouldn't switch on.

"Are you kidding me?" Jared said out loud. He shook it to see if it would come to life, but it didn't help. "Do you have a camera?" he asked the girl, but she said no. He took off his gloves and cupped the camera in his hands. "Maybe if I can warm it up, it'll come back to life."

"Hurry! I'm really cold," she said, and pulled her hood down a little farther over her face, trying to shield it from the wind.

The cold air blasted them for five full bitterly cold minutes before the camera booted back to life. Jared took a photo, and then a few more, to be on the safe side. The two of them smiled big for the photo, and they meant it. They were on the top of Mount Rainier! They'd done a really challenging thing under very bad circumstances—and they'd made it. They had every right to be proud.

"Let's get out of here," Jared said, as he put his camera back in his bag.

Jared and Diane on the Summit.

US Geological Survey Marker at Mt Rainier summit, 14,411 feet, August 31, 2010.

The weather would not relent.

They climbed back over the crater's rim the way they'd entered it and felt the wind blasting snow at them from across the entire expanse of glacier. The snow had once again turned to ice and was whipping through the wind, pelting Jared's face like a barrage of BBs.

It's easy to assume that climbing down the mountain would be less difficult than climbing up, because on the way down, at least you're not fighting to push your body weight up against gravity. In practice, though, climbing down can be at least as hard: that downward pull of gravity means your body has to spend energy to slow itself down, to keep from falling. The climb down puts a lot more stress on the joints, especially the knees.

And, of course, one misstep, and you slide off the mountain.

On top of that, they had been climbing for eight hours. They were both in great shape, but that didn't mean they weren't getting tired—tired physically and also tired mentally of the meticulous monotony, step after each slow step, having to be careful and alert even in the midst of so much repetition.

How long would it be back to Mikk, who was waiting to meet up with them? And from there, how long would it take to get back to base camp? Four more hours like this? Five?

Longer, if the weather stayed this bad.

But there was nothing else to do. They kept climbing down through the swirling snow and hail, following the intermittent orange flags that marked their path, and each time they arrived at one, they'd scout out the next one down the hill, and then inch their way down to that one. Progress was slow, but at least it was foolproof. Or so they'd thought until the orange flags led them straight to the edge of a giant crevasse, bigger by far than anything they'd seen on the way up, so wide across they could hardly even see to its other side.

"What is this?" the girl asked. "Did we cross this on the way up?"

Jared looked around. Had this chasm opened up *while they were on the summit?* No, that didn't seem possible. It was too big! A break this big would have been catastrophic, would have caused avalanches, would have been impossible to miss.

So then, how could it be here? There's no chance they had crossed this crevasse—was it even a crevasse?—on the way up; he would have remembered it for sure.

He had a sinking suspicion that what they were looking at was the "bergschrund" of the Ingraham Glacier, the enormous crack at the glacier's top that separates it from the old, brittle ice of the summit. He stared down into the unfathomably deep chasm, and couldn't think of any possible way to cross it.

But worse than that: this was something they hadn't seen before.

They had not come across the bergschrund on their path up the mountain.

That meant they were taking the wrong way down.

"We must be on the wrong path," Jared said to the girl.

"What does that mean, 'the wrong path'? We've been following the flags the whole way."

"I don't know. They must have been the wrong flags."

The wrong flags. He hadn't even considered this possibility as they came down off the summit. As far as he'd known, there should only be one set of flags.

But somewhere on the way down, the path must have forked, and they'd missed it and taken the wrong fork without knowing, and it had led them to this, the bergschrund: a dead end.

"We have to climb back up," he said.

"Up?"

"We need to see if we can find where we got off our path."

It was depressing news, but they had no choice. Reluctantly, they started back up the mountain again.

CHAPTER
EIGHT

AUGUST 31, 2010

10:00 A.M.

Diane wasn't sure if she preferred climbing up the mountain or down the mountain, but one thing she did not like was climbing up and down and up and down, over and over.

After they'd come to that chasm and realized they were off the path, they climbed up again for—how long? Hard to say. It was getting harder and harder to keep track of time: the sun was out, but barely: the squalling wind, snow, and clouds blocked most of its light. And Diane's exhausted legs and mind were putting her into a trancelike state.

Had it been minutes? Hours?

They'd gone up the mountain for a while, looking for more orange flags, or footprints, or any indication of where they might have missed a turn. They tried heading down what they thought was a footpath of trodden snow, only to discover, after some time, that this, too, was a dead end.

And then they climbed back up again.

Standing by one of the flags—one of the bad flags—they scanned the glacier, looking for a flag or a path or . . . *anything*.

They were on a giant sheet of ice with no landmarks.

She yanked the bamboo pole out of the snow

"What are you doing?" Jared asked.

"It's useless anyway! It shouldn't even be here." Then she looked at the flag in her hand and stuffed it into her backpack. "And this way, I get a souvenir."

A souvenir of the time I got lost on Mount Rainier, she thought to herself. But she didn't want to say that word out loud, "lost." She and Jared weren't lost. They were just a little turned around. They would find the way down soon enough.

Jared looked at the bamboo pole she'd tossed in her pack and it seemed to give him an idea.

"Maybe one of the flags from our path blew down in the weather," he said. It was possible. The wind was intense, and snow this high on Rainier was expected this time of the year, covering up any flag that might have fallen, erasing any footprints that previous groups might have left behind. "Maybe the flag we're looking for is lying flat on the ground."

They looked out again across the ice. If the flag that pointed to their path had blown over, there was no chance they'd see it out here now in this weather. How much snow had fallen in the past few hours and had been tossed about with the gusting winds? More than enough to cover a short bamboo pole on the ground and hide it from their view.

Diane thought of her mom, who was quite apprehensive of her

daughter joining this expedition. "Every year, ten thousand people climb Mount Rainier!" she'd reassured her mother . . . and herself.

Diane also knew, but hadn't said, that every year, a few people die on the mountain.

It's a statistic—an unlucky handful of people who get caught in the wrong place at the wrong time—an experienced team lost in a fluke avalanche, or an unfortunate soul who falls through a snow bridge into a crevasse.

You never think you might actually *become* one of those people.

The wind blew a fresh gust of snow into her face and jolted her out of her thought, and then she saw . . .

"What's that?" she asked Jared. "Do you see that, down to the right?"

She pointed down the glacier. In the distance, on the other side of a small crevasse, there were a few upright shapes. Moving.

"Are those people?" she asked.

Of all the lucky breaks! She and Jared took off down the glacier toward these other climbers. Now it didn't matter if they found their way back to their original trail or not. After all, more than a half-dozen climbing routes went from Camp Muir to the summit, and any one of these would be able to lead them back to their friends and then get them home.

They were going to be all right.

To get to the other climbers, she and Jared first had to get around that small crevasse. That would slow them down a little, and take them a little out of their way, but by now, the two of them had crossed a dozen crevasses together. This additional one shouldn't be any real trouble.

They hiked up and around it and then scanned the glacier again for that team of climbers. Diane worried a little about losing them in the snow and low visibility. But she spied the distant shapes, and she and Jared raced down the ice after them. They went as fast as they could, maybe even too fast; they weren't paying especially close attention to any possible dangers. Diane realized in her haste that she might be walking across unseen snow bridges, or might lose her footing on some weak ice. And the path down was steeper than she would have liked. But she didn't care. It seemed more important to go fast and catch up to those climbers before they disappeared from view.

It was hard to judge distances on the glacier. The lack of landmarks meant there wasn't much basis for eyeballing an estimate. Everything was farther than she'd guessed it to be. She and Jared were moving at their quickest tempo in hours, but still, they barely seemed to be getting closer.

"What if they're hiking down faster than we are?" she asked Jared. "Then we'll never catch up."

He thought about this.

"I don't think it matters if we catch them or not. As long as we can find the path they're on, we're golden. We'll follow them the rest of the way down to base camp, whether they know we're here or not."

"If they save our lives, then we'll owe them a drink." Diane smiled. "Did you guys save any of that Goldschläger?"

Did she notice first, or did Jared? The shapes weren't moving after all. The closer they got, the more undeniable it became. The shapes weren't moving.

The shapes weren't even climbers.

They were rocks—rocks and shadows and ice, and tricks of the light, and wishful thinking. She and Jared had just raced what seemed like a half mile downhill off whatever semblance of a path they might have been on, to chase after a set of rocks.

Great.

A set of rocks.

She couldn't believe it.

Where were they? Where was the path? How were they going to get home?

She sat down on the ice.

"What are we going to do?" she whispered.

The wind blew, and Jared scanned the ice above and below, but he didn't answer.

"What are we going to do?" Diane asked again, trying not to scream, trying not to cry.

"I don't know! I don't know! Why are you asking me?"

"Because, Jared, you're the one with the experience here! You're the one in the Air Force, with survival training. You're the one who knows about belays and carabiners and all that. You're the one who told Dan I'd be okay! So what's the plan? What are we going to do?"

Jared took a breath and looked around again.

"I think we have to go down."

She couldn't believe what she was hearing.

"That's your plan? We have to 'go down'?"

"Yeah. We have to go down."

"I know we have to go down, Jared! We're on a mountain that we don't want to be on any longer. The only logical way to go is down!"

He looked at her sheepishly. She hadn't seen him look sheepish before, and she immediately felt bad for yelling at him. She remembered her first impression of Jared as arrogant and cocky, and then she remembered too that she'd misread that, at least partly: that he was also maybe a bit shy.

"I don't know the path back to Camp Muir," he said. "I can't even guess what direction to go. But I know the weather keeps getting worse, and I know we have to get off this mountain. So the only thing

I can think to do is go down. If we climb down the glacier, any way we can, then we'll get to the tree line. We'll get out of this cold, maybe out of this storm. We'll have more options, if we just go down."

"Just down?"

"The best we can. We find our way around the crevasses and rocky cliffs, and we keep aiming down."

It wasn't much of a plan, but it was the best plan they had.

"Okay," she agreed. "Let's go down."

CHAPTER
NINE

AUGUST 31, 2010

2:00 P.M.

*H*ow long can you go without food?

Jared was remembering some things he'd learned in survival training, and doing some calculating.

It takes a body weeks, roughly three weeks, to starve to death. But what about energy? It wasn't starving he was worried about; it was keeping their energy up long enough to climb off this mountain. How much fuel would they need to keep up their energy?

How many calories do you burn mountain climbing?

Who knows. Maybe 500 an hour? Maybe more? It costs the body a lot of energy to keep warm. How long had they been out here? Ten hours? So, 5,000 calories? Had they eaten 5,000 calories since they'd left? Not even close. He remembered eating a bag of almonds and raisins, but that was hours ago. And how far were they from

Camp Muir—most optimistic estimate, if they got lucky? Another five hours? Another 2,500 calories?

Did they have another 2,500 calories in their packs—each?

No way. Between them, they had a couple pieces of dried kiwi and a small handful of trail mix.

The question he couldn't get out of his mind, though, was this:

How much water do you need to survive?

More than they had.

When they'd given the last of their drinking water to Mikk— when was that, seven hours ago?—all their remaining water was frozen rock solid in their water bottles. They'd moved the bottles into their coats to thaw them out and give them a fresh supply of drinking water.

But it hadn't worked. Their water was still frozen solid. Neither one of them had consumed even a sip of water in seven hours.

It was strange, being surrounded in every direction by water— but all of it undrinkable because it was frozen solid. They say hiking on a glacier is like hiking in the desert: *intense* due to the dehydrating sun and no running water. And if there is running water on a glacier, it is buried deep below the surface of the ice. In a desert, the heat tells the body that it's drying out. But on a glacier, in the cold, the sun saps your fluid without your even noticing.

One advantage of a glacier is that, of course, it's made of water. Mountaineers can always cut away some ice or scoop up some snow, melt it with their camp stoves, and drink up.

Too bad Jared had left his camp stove at Camp Muir.

At the time—only half a day ago, though it seemed like weeks— nothing had seemed more important than lightening their packs, cutting all unnecessary weight to help increase their chances of making it to the summit. No camp stove, Jared had decided. His little gas stove was just a quarter of a pound, but he'd decided he didn't want to bother with its weight.

Water, water everywhere—but not a drop to drink.

He realized their frozen water bottles weighed so much more than his camp stove. They even weighed more than his tent, which he'd also chosen to leave behind.

No matter. None of that mattered. All that mattered was getting down, pressing on down the mountain.

Jared did his best to chart a path down the glacier. It wasn't easy. They were facing more crevasses, usually a few feet wide, with no choice but to jump over them. In other spots, their path led them to almost vertical drops. If he could see a way to do it, and if the bottom of the drop-off looked like a promising path, then he would set up a rope and they would climb down—which took a lot of time and a lot of energy.

But almost as often, he would look at the drop and decide it was impassable. It was too steep, too far, too unsafe. Or it didn't seem to lead anywhere except into more danger. When this happened, he would turn them around and they would climb back up the path they'd come down until they found a different, hopefully more promising way down.

It was almost pure guesswork, but Jared tried to keep his spirits up. He knew that if they were persistent, then they would find their way down. He believed it, even if he didn't know for sure. He pretended to believe it, even if deep down inside, he had his doubts.

They came to a steep section that was littered with loose rocks. He didn't like the look of it one bit. There was no good way to anchor his rope. The handholds were terrible and there wasn't enough ice to rely on the crampons. But he couldn't see another way to go.

"It's only about twenty feet," he said to the girl. "I think we can do it."

"Do what?" she asked.

She'd been a good sport so far, but he could see she was fading. He was pretty sure that if he'd had a mirror, he could look in it and see that he was fading too.

"Climb down," he said. "So what do you think?"

She peered over the edge.

"I don't think it occurred to me to be nervous until you asked me what I think."

He decided she should go first. That way, he could harness her to his rope and anchor himself at the top, so he would be able to catch her if she slipped. When they found a spot and had the belay set up, she moved to the edge of the drop and peered down.

"You'll be fine," Jared told her.

"I'm not sure how to start," she explained.

He smiled, hoping to encourage her.

"One step at a time."

She sat on the ledge and then found her first foothold in the ice.

"Okay, I'm going," she said.

"Belay ready," he called back, and dug his crampons into the ice for more support as she dropped down over the edge of the drop and out of sight.

"I'm down!" she shouted a couple minutes later.

Now it was his turn. He was more nervous than he had let on; he would have to do the same climb down, but without the protection of a person supporting him with a belay. It was free-climbing under terrible conditions. It wasn't that far to the bottom, and if he were less tired, less cold, less frustrated, less lost, then he probably wouldn't have been worried at all.

But under these circumstances? If something happened to him, if he slipped and fell, if he broke an ankle or worse, then they were both in trouble. And he knew it.

It's okay, he told himself. *You've got this.*

"One step at a time!" the girl called out, echoing his own words of encouragement. And that's how he climbed his way to the bottom: one step at a time.

They did this a few more times, down a series of small drops. He would let her down first with a belay, and once she was safely at the bottom, he would carefully do another short free-climb. They were spending a lot of energy—and time!—making it through this section, but Jared didn't see any other way.

Finally they came to a flatter stretch of glacier and Jared was able to put his climbing rope back inside his bag, at least for now. It was a relief to get to a section of glacier that was more straightforward, a simple icy walk downhill. But coming out of the steep section also exposed them to more wind and snow. There was nearly a foot of fresh snow on the ground, and trudging through it was exhausting.

They clambered down the glacier, poking at the ground with their ice axes so they didn't wind up on a weak ice bridge, and hopping over the small crevasses. It seemed routine by now. How many times had they done this today?

But there was no doubt they were running out of steam—and, it turned out, running out of luck too: the downward climb they'd been on for the past half hour or so ended, suddenly, in a precipitous dead end.

Jared looked around for a possible path down or around and didn't see either.

"All right, this is no good. Let's head back up."

But she shook her head.

"No."

"No? What do you mean, 'no'?"

"I don't want to go back up."

Jared took a moment to make sure he understood her correctly.

"This crevasse is impossible to cross. What do you want us to do?"

But she sat down on the ice and wouldn't budge.

"Our plan was to go down, so I'm going down. I'm not going up anymore. Promise me?"

"Promise you what?"

"Promise me we won't have to go up anymore."

What she was saying didn't make any sense. But he could see that, right now, there wasn't much point in arguing, so he sat down next to her.

"Let's rest here a bit."

Jared looked at her. Even here, on what was probably the worst day of their lives, she was beautiful. He didn't want to lie to her; he knew they'd have to go uphill sooner or later. But he didn't have the heart to give her any bad news. So he sat beside her quietly.

"What am I doing here?" she asked. "I shouldn't even be here. I can't believe this is happening. I can't believe this is happening!"

She was breathing in fast, short gasps, a little out of control. Jared put his hands on her shoulders to try and calm her, and looked her in the eye.

"Hey, listen to me. I can't promise you that we won't have to go uphill anymore. But stay calm, keep a level head, and I promise you this: I will get you off this mountain. Okay?"

"Okay."

CHAPTER
TEN

It seemed endless, one crevasse after another after another. How many crevasses could there be? How big was this glacier?

How big was this mountain?

Diane didn't know how much more of this she could take. They trudged in silence, mostly. Even if they'd had the energy to talk, it would have been impossible to hear each other over the roar of wind. There wasn't anything to say. There wasn't even anything to think.

There was just one foot in front of the other. Try not to slip; try not to fall. Try to keep going.

Whenever they came to a new crevasse, they would stop to test the strength of the ice in front of them, checking to make sure that what they thought was the crevasse edge was not, in fact, a thin layer of snow that would collapse underneath them. They would poke at it hard with the spike of their axes until they were confident it would hold their weight, and then they would step up to the edge to decide whether or not they could jump over. Most of the crevasses were about two feet across, which was manageable.

The crevasse in front of them was closer to three feet across. The difference between jumping two feet and jumping three feet felt infinitely vast to her right now. Three feet, while wearing all this gear, seemed impossible.

But there was no other choice. The only way forward was to make the impossible possible.

She took off her backpack and felt her body lengthen, no longer pushed downward by all the extra weight. It felt good to be free of the pack. She felt like, without the pack, she could certainly jump three feet. Without the pack, she felt like she could fly.

"Hey, Jared," she said. "What if I throw my pack over to the other side? Will you catch it and make sure it doesn't slide?"

He nodded and carefully jumped across the crevasse so he'd be ready to catch her pack when she threw it.

She picked the pack up. It was heavy, but not that heavy, and she hurled it across the open maw of the crevasse. It sailed over easily— and then she followed it by jumping.

This would work, she realized. Anytime the jump seemed like it might be too far, she could toss the pack across first.

With this new tactic, she managed the next set of crevasses more confidently, pausing only long enough to take off her pack, toss it across, and then jump over. No more hesitating at the edge, wondering whether or not she'd be able to make the jump. No more pausing for self-doubt. They were making good time, now that she'd found this new rhythm, or so it seemed to her. This was kind of easy, really.

That's when her foot slipped.

No, it wasn't her foot. Her foot was anchored to the ice beneath her with a crampon. What slipped was the ice itself, underneath her foot: it broke off and collapsed into the crevasse. Diane quickly leaned backward away from the crevasse and put all of her weight into her back foot, watching as the ground beneath her front foot vanished into the pit of blue ice.

She had almost fallen. If she'd been an inch or two farther up, if she'd been leaning forward a little more, she would have gone in for sure. She would be at the bottom of that crevasse, along with that collapsed ice.

"I can't," she said. "I can't." She didn't even know specifically what she meant she couldn't do. Any of it. She couldn't keep pretending to be optimistic. They were alone on this frozen mountain.

Jared stood on the other side of the crevasse, watching her. She wasn't sure if he had seen how close she'd been to falling in—but he didn't chastise her or try to rush her. He waited patiently while she dug around inside her heart to find a little more courage, and then she got up and jumped and made it to the other side.

When she got there, he nodded at her. Maybe he was too tired to say much. Maybe he knew there wasn't much to say. But she got the sense that he was proud of her, for persevering, and she was proud of herself too.

She had heard the term "whiteout" before, and she had always thought it was another way to describe a heavy snowfall—but now that she was in one, she understood what the term truly meant.

The ice beneath her and the sky above her and the clouds and falling snow around her were all the exact same color. There was no way to tell which was which. The entire world around her was white. It felt like she was floating inside a giant white room with no north or south, with no up or down. It was amazingly dangerous.

This was how they had come to the edge of a steep, icy cliff and almost walked right over it without noticing: because the air in front of them looked exactly the same as the ground beneath them.

"Jared!" she cried out, stopping him before he walked off the edge.

"Wow," he said. "Thanks."

They stood a few inches from the cliff and looked down. It was maybe forty feet to the bottom.

"We have to get down that somehow."

For once, she didn't argue.

Jared brushed off some of the recent snowfall to expose red rock underneath. He kicked it hard with his crampon to test its strength, and it crumbled.

"Is that . . . ?" Diane trailed off. "I don't know anything about rock climbing, but, is that safe?"

"It'll be fine," he said, though she didn't know if he was lying to make her feel better. "I'll belay you down, same as before."

"But what about you? This is way higher than the others. Is there a way we can belay you too?"

Jared rubbed his hands together to warm them up, but didn't say anything. Then he dug around in his pack, pulled out a helmet, and put it on.

"What's that for?" she asked.

"It's a helmet," he said, not quite answering.

He's worried, Diane realized. She hadn't seen Jared scared yet, even after all they'd been through. Or anyway, she hadn't seen him show it. If he had been scared at any point, then he was very good at keeping it on the inside.

She could tell that this time was different. She still wouldn't have described him as scared, exactly—but he looked very concerned.

"Are you sure about this?" she asked him.

"Let's go."

Jared got on the ground and dug his crampons into the snow to anchor himself for the belay, and Diane climbed down, picking her way through the flaky rocks. Her part in this was easy: even if she slipped and lost her footing, Jared would catch her. But what about his turn? What would happen if he slipped while climbing down? What then?

She did her best to hurry to the bottom so Jared wouldn't spend too much energy on the belay, or get too cold or stiff sitting up there waiting for her.

"Okay!" she yelled. "I'm down!"

A few moments later, she saw his leg stretch down over the ledge, followed by the other, and he began climbing down, using both of their ice axes as he had done on the previous vertical sections.

"You're doing great!" she called up, not knowing how else to help.

Every time he planted his foot, a steady shower of red rock crumbled down the wall, and she watched it, knowing it meant the entire rock was fragile, and that any one of his toeholds could collapse.

"You're about halfway!" she shouted. "Not much farther now!"

On one section of the wall, he paused, not seeing a clear next step, and as he held in place, she could see his legs starting to shake.

"You can do this, Jared. Ten more feet."

Somewhere in that last stretch, he lost his footing, or maybe decided to jump, but suddenly he was coming down much faster than he'd planned, and he thudded down on some angled rock at the bottom.

"Ow!" he grunted.

She rushed over to him.

"Are you okay?"

He stood up and held his ankle.

"Yeah. Yeah, I'm okay. I banged up my shin pretty bad. But I'm fine." He limped away from the rock, and she wondered if he truly was fine, or if he was just saying that for her sake.

How much longer could they go on?

CHAPTER
ELEVEN

AUGUST 31, 2010

5:00 P.M.

"Down there," Jared pointed. "Do you see it?" He could barely keep the excitement out of his voice.

They stood at the edge of an icy ravine of sorts, looking out into a valley below them, the first clear view they'd had in hours.

"I'm not sure. Where?"

He tried pointing it out to her.

"Follow that ridgeline down, and then, a little to the right, that flat bit—that's a pond. Right? A frozen pond. And if you look close, see those two spots? Way back, on the other side?"

"Are those people?"

He nodded.

"I think those are people! Two people."

"Wow. Okay. Wow." She squinted again, trying to get a clearer view. "What are they doing out there? Why are they sitting on a frozen pond?"

"I don't know, maybe they're ice fishing. Who cares what they're doing? They're people! They'll have cell phones. They'll have a map." Jared hadn't felt this good in hours. "You see that shape behind them, that black rectangle? My guess is, that's a snowmobile."

"Wow," she said again. "A snowmobile! I mean, wow."

"Right?"

"How far is it, do you think?"

He shrugged.

"What is that, maybe a half mile?" he said.

"A snowmobile! Hey, this is kind of bad, but when we get down there, what if I tell them I have a neck injury or something? If we tell them I have a broken neck, they'll have to give us a ride back to camp, right?"

He laughed, though he wasn't sure if she was entirely joking.

She cupped her hands around her mouth and shouted as loud as she could: "HELLOOOO!!!"

Jared joined her: "Hey! Over here!!!"

They jumped up and down and waved their arms and tried to get the attention of the fishermen, but it was of no use. They were too far and there was still too much wind.

"We have to get closer," Jared said.

Easier said than done. Before they could reach the pond, before they could reach the ice fishermen and their snowmobile, before they could finally return to safety, the two of them had to get down this ravine.

They had done a lot of climbing already that day, up and down crevasses and ice cliffs and some steep sections of rock, but this was different. This was a whole ravine, a mini canyon that dropped fifty feet or so below them and then funneled down the mountain like a giant icy slide, eventually—steeply—spilling out onto the plain, closer to the fishermen.

They had two possible ways down and neither one was very good. The first option was a long, narrow ice bridge that spanned the canyon and would take them to the opposite side, which sloped more gently than the side they were on, and which would allow them to climb carefully down to the plain.

But they didn't like the look of the ice bridge, which narrowed in the middle to no more than six inches wide. It's not that hard balancing on a six-inch bridge—unless you're carrying a giant backpack, dangling over a fifty-foot fall, in the wind, and you've been exhausting your legs for the past seventeen hours straight, and the bridge is made of ice. One misstep from this ice bridge would mean taking a very bad fall. And Jared wasn't completely sure the bridge would even hold their weight in its narrowest spot.

The other path down was right in front of them: they could climb straight down the steep, icy side of the ravine. They had done smaller-scale versions of this climb all morning, Jared setting up a belay while she climbed down, and then following behind her. But this was way too far to free-climb. He wasn't even sure his rope would be long enough to belay her all the way to the bottom.

"We have to do the ice bridge," he told her. "It's the only way."

"You're joking. We can't walk across that. That's insane."

"Well we can't climb down this wall! *That's* insane."

She started shouting at the fishermen again, hoping maybe this time they would hear. But it was to no avail.

"What if— Can we belay each other while we each walk across the bridge? So if one of us falls, the other will catch them?"

Jared shook his head.

"It's a good idea in theory. But if one of us falls, they're gonna yank the other person down after them."

"Okay, but—we have to get down somehow."

"I know."

"I mean, what if while we're stuck up here, the fishermen decide to call it a day and go home? We have to get down there," she said.

"I know!" Jared racked his brain, trying to think of a solution. All these hours of climbing, not eating, not drinking—it was all getting to him. He needed his mind to work a little bit longer. "What if . . ."

"Say it."

"I'm thinking, I can belay you straight down into the ravine—if the rope is long enough—and then I'll take my chances on the ice bridge and climb down the other side."

"You mean split up?"

He nodded. He couldn't think of another way.

Jared set up the belay spot and helped her down over the ledge. Because of a lip in the ice, as soon as she climbed over the edge, she vanished from his view. They called out to each other, her telling him when she needed him to feed out more rope—but before long, he couldn't hear her. He tried to gauge her progress by watching his rope. Whenever there was tension, he would let out a little more slack so she could climb down a little farther.

"Hey!" he called out. "How's it going?"

But if she answered, he never heard it.

He didn't know what to do. Was she all right? He couldn't get up to look without giving up his position anchoring her. Checking on her would put her in danger. He had to trust she was doing okay. As long as there was tension on the line, that meant she was still safely climbing down.

At least, that's what he hoped.

But he was running out of rope. *Coming to the end of my rope,* he thought to himself, and laughed. He'd never thought about that expression quite so literally.

"Are you at the bottom?"

Still no answer.

He tugged at the rope to test its tension. It seemed slack, too slack to be bearing her weight. That meant one of two things: either she'd made it to the bottom and detached from the rope—and didn't need him belaying her anymore—or she was perched somewhere on the side of the ravine, resting or stuck—and absolutely still needed him where he was.

He didn't know what to do.

"Hey!" he called out again.

He had only a couple feet of rope left. That meant she'd already climbed down a distance equal to the rope's length—and if his estimate of the ravine's height had been even close to accurate, that meant she had to be at the bottom by now, or at least very close to the bottom.

Right?

There was no way to be sure. He had to decide: Should he stay where he was, holding the belay? Or was it safe for him to move on?

That's when he saw her, already in the distance, at the bottom of the ravine, heading up the other side. She was moving faster than he'd seen her move in hours, racing off in the direction of the ice fishermen.

Wow, he thought. *She's not wasting any time.* "Thanks for all your help," she was probably thinking. "Now if you'll excuse me, I have a snowmobile to catch."

He laughed again. Maybe he was getting a little loopy.

In any case, he'd better catch up.

The ice bridge was even narrower than he had guessed. *This is way too risky.* He stopped, looked up the mountain, and selected a different spot with a more gradual slope to downclimb and reunite with his climbing partner. After making sure all his backpack straps were tight, Jared tossed his bag down the slope and climbed down to it.

When he made it to the other side, he let out a giant lungful of air. He planted both feet on the ground. He'd made it.

From here, the rest of the walk was straightforward: he just had to hike up the sloping side of the ravine and meet up with the girl.

Because of the angle of the hill, he wouldn't be able to see her until he'd made it all the way to the top of the other side and out onto the open plain. He expected her to be a quarter of a mile away by now, with the head start she'd gotten and how quickly she'd been racing. But when he saw her, she was standing still, only a hundred feet away.

That's sweet, he thought. *She waited for me.*

It was only as he got closer that he realized that wasn't why she'd stopped.

She'd stopped because the ice fishermen weren't ice fishermen, the snowmobile wasn't a snowmobile, and the pond wasn't a pond. They were more rocks and ice, more optical illusions, and more dashed hopes. They were nothing.

The sun was beginning to set, and they were still lost on Mount Rainier.

CHAPTER
TWELVE

D iane didn't know what to do.

This wasn't a subject that was ever covered in school: "How to Survive When You're Lost on a Glacier." She racked her brain, trying to think of every class she had ever taken, all those required subjects in exercise physiology and human performance, and she couldn't think of how a single one of them was useful to her right now. She remembered the metabolic cost of using ice was greater than the hydration gained, but screw the equations; she needed water.

She'd been eating mouthfuls of snow, but they didn't seem to help one bit with the thirst she was feeling. It wasn't her mouth that was thirsty. It was her entire body, all its muscles, all its bones. She felt like a wrung-out sponge that would be able to soak up a lake full of water.

But there were no lakes here—just endless ice.

Higher up, there had been—or so she'd been told—a small crater lake, the highest lake in North America. Not that she had seen it. She hadn't been able to see anything from the summit, thanks to the thick clouds, the wind, and the snow.

What a stupid idea this trip had been: to climb Mount Rainier in the dark, in the snow, to see nothing. To get stuck on the mountain without even a single decent photo. To get stuck on the mountain at all.

Jared was building them a place to sleep, bless him. He inventoried their backpacks and found that they had two sleeping bags, a tarp, and a lightweight snow shovel, and he set about carving them a little nook in the ice. When he first started digging, he said something ambitious about wanting to build them an igloo—but after a few minutes of fighting with his little shovel to cut into the frozen, wind-packed snow, he gave up on that plan and settled for a more modest one: a ditch, six feet long, four feet wide, and maybe a foot and a half deep. They could put their sleeping bags inside, he said, and lay the tarp on top of them, and sleep through the night, insulated and shielded from the wind.

It was a good plan, though she couldn't stop thinking that the ditch looked like a grave. *Will a search party find us here, frozen, in the morning? Will they find us at all?*

She watched Jared, still toiling away. He was anchoring a corner of the tarp to the ditch with his ice axe; he used her axe to secure a second corner. So resourceful. She was grateful for him. He was relentlessly positive and pragmatic, incapable of pessimism. Like a battery-powered Boy Scout. She didn't know what she would have done without him.

Died, she guessed.

No. She would have turned around with Dan and Amber, all

those hours ago, and been perfectly safe and sound.

Who knows?

She and Jared had disagreed at first about whether even to set up camp for the night. He'd wanted to keep walking, at least while there was any glint of daylight, and maybe even after the sun was down.

"We have to get lower," he kept saying.

But they came to another crevasse, this one much larger than any of the others they had stumbled on earlier in the day, too wide to cross, and that meant they weren't going to get any lower, not tonight. They were going to have to hike back uphill again, the way they came.

They had already been hiking for almost twenty hours, and during those twenty hours, they had escaped death an uncountable number of times. She didn't want to do it anymore. She didn't want to climb uphill again. She didn't want to face more danger. She wanted to stop walking. She wanted to lie down and sleep, and then be rescued when she woke up in the morning.

It wasn't impossible that they would be rescued. Dan and the others had expected them back at Camp Muir by 1:00 p.m. That was six hours ago. By now, people knew they were missing and were worried about them, at the very least. It seemed likely that there were people already out searching for them—hikers and helicopters and climbing rangers, people with vast experience making rescues on the mountain. Maybe by tomorrow everything would be okay. They just had to stay alive until tomorrow.

She grabbed another handful of snow and put it in her mouth.

"Hey," Jared said. "I think it's ready."

He walked her over to give her a tour of their accommodations for the night. It was just a ditch in the ice, and, yes, it looked like a grave, but she couldn't wait to lie down in it. She had never been this tired in her life.

Right as he was about to show her the little ledge he'd carved out as extra protection for their heads from the elements—she accidentally stepped on it and smashed it. She saw a few emotions flicker across his face in rapid succession: surprise, anger, disappointment. It was as close as she'd come to seeing him get mad. But it wasn't her fault! How was she supposed to know that he had built them an "ice roof"?

He ushered her back out of the ditch and tried to repair the little ledge, but soon gave up. Then he unzipped her sleeping bag as far as he could (the mummy-shaped bags were designed not to unzip fully, leaving the shape of the bottom intact and able to hold the user's feet). He laid it out like a mattress and unzipped his own bag so they could use it as a comforter. No bed had ever looked as inviting as this little ditch in the ice. She wanted so badly to lie down, stretch out, take all the weight off her tired legs and back.

I just met this guy yesterday, she thought. *And now I'm sleeping with him!* She laughed, but she couldn't tell if she was laughing on the inside or out loud. Whatever—it didn't matter. What mattered was sleep. She walked back to their "house" and climbed into their "bed."

"Stop, stop!" Jared shouted. He was looking at her feet, where her crampons were about to tear the down-filled sleeping bags to shreds.

Oops.

She reached down and tried to unclip the binding on her crampon, but it was stuck. Or maybe her fingers were stuck. Something was stuck.

Jared saw the trouble she was having.

"Let me help you."

He unfastened the bindings and her crampons fell to the ground. Then she passed out from exhaustion.

Diane awoke in the middle of the night. Was it the middle of the night? It was so hard to tell. Everything was dark and suffocating, pitch black all around her. She couldn't breathe. Where was she? Why wasn't there air? She waved her hand at the darkness in front of her face and felt the tarp, heavy with new snow and pushing down on top of them.

Smothering us, she thought.

She pushed up at the tarp to shake off the snow.

"What are you doing?" Jared asked.

"It was choking me," she explained.

"The snow is an insulator. It keeps the heat in."

"I couldn't breathe." She tried to sit up and found her feet were stuck inside the bottom of the sleeping bag. She still had her boots on, and the bulk of them, plus Jared's feet, filled up the bottom of the mummy-shaped bag. "Sorry," she apologized, for disrupting him while trying to get her feet out. Then she lifted her corner of the tarp.

"What's happening?" he asked.

"I have to pee."

She got up to pee three times during the night. It was driving Jared crazy. He didn't seem to be getting any sleep at all, and every time she got up and climbed out of their little shelter, it wiped out whatever heat they'd managed to accumulate underneath.

"You haven't had any water in sixteen hours!" he said.

"I'm sorry!" She couldn't explain why she had to pee. She just had to pee.

After the second time, Jared sat up, wide awake.

"I think we should get going," he said.

"What? Why?" She couldn't believe he was even suggesting this. It was the middle of the night. If they were going to get rescued, or find a trail, or find anything at all, then they needed daylight. "We're sort of warm here. We're safe. There's not one good reason for us to leave right now."

"My feet are freezing, and I can't stare up at this tarp for another five hours until sunrise."

"Then go to sleep!" she said.

"I can't sleep! I haven't slept one minute. I think we should get up and start moving. The sooner we get back to climbing, the sooner we'll get off this mountain."

She saw he was stir-crazy, maybe still hopped up on the adrenaline that had been fueling him—and saving them both—all day long.

"Listen! Do you hear that wind? The storm is still raging outside. It's dumping down snow like crazy, covering up the crevasses that we know are in every direction. We need to wait here until sunrise."

"I can't wait that long," he replied. "I'll go crazy!"

"Please, Jared. I can't do this without you, and you can't do it if you don't get a little rest. Sunrise—okay?"

He was still restless, but he was thinking about it, at least.

"Okay," he finally answered.

Then Diane threw aside the tarp and the wind blasted in.

"What are you doing?" Jared groaned.

"I have to pee again."

When she got back, she didn't know if he was asleep or pretending to be asleep for her sake.

"Good night," she whispered—softly, so she wouldn't wake him.

CHAPTER
THIRTEEN

It was the longest night of Jared's life. And the slowest. And probably the coldest. When he had first laid down, he could feel the muscles of his body tingling, especially in his legs. He'd been using them for so many hours in a row, it was like they didn't want to stop. They prickled with electricity and made him restless.

His mind was still spinning too, coming up with plans and strategies—thinking about paths around this first crevasse, trying to imagine where they might be on the mountain, how long until they might find running water, what they might do to increase the odds of rescue.

He kept getting stuck on "If only"—if only they could build a signal fire, if only they could get below the tree line, if only the water in their CamelBaks and Nalgene bottles would thaw from their body heat. If only so many things. Then his mind would turn to another set of "If onlys"—the missteps they'd made: if only he had packed his stove so they could melt some snow into drinking water. If only one of them had brought a GPS or cell phone or radio.

If only they had turned around when everyone else on the mountain did, instead of marching stubbornly up to the summit and into the heart of the storm.

Still, they'd come up against a lot of adversities and, one by one, they had overcome each of them. He had spent nights bivouacked on mountains before, and this wasn't so different from those other times: cold, yes. Uncomfortable, for sure.

Survivable? Certainly.

He looked at his watch. He would wait for what felt like hours before checking it again, only to discover it had been a few excruciatingly long minutes. He watched the seconds tick by in slow motion. He watched them count up, and up, and up.

One minute.

Finally.

Then he'd watch as it ticked through a second minute.

How is it possible that time is moving this slowly?

The storm continued to rage, dumping inches more snow on top of them. As he'd told the girl, the snow was good for insulation, but he hadn't expected it to pile up so fast. Jared pounded the snow with his fists to clear it off the tarp periodically so it wouldn't suffocate them.

Outside, the snow obscured all vision. It made sense of direction impossible and it made any chance of rescue unlikely. No helicopter was going to fly in this weather, at this altitude, and even if it did, no one would be able to spot them down here, in the blizzard, in the dark.

He thought about their gear, wondering how visible any of it might be from the air: their parkas, pants, and packs were mostly white, blue, and black: glacier colored. If they'd been trying to dress in snow camouflage, they couldn't have done a better job.

He couldn't feel his feet. The girl had wedged her feet inside the mummy bag, boots and all, and he might've done the same, but there was no way to get his boots to fit in too—so he'd removed them for the night. It felt good, at first, letting his toes stretch, letting his feet air out and breathe inside his Gore-Tex socks. But after a little while, he felt them tingling from the cold, and then after a while longer, he noticed he didn't feel them tingling anymore. He didn't feel them at all anymore.

That wasn't good.

He sat up and rubbed them to see if he could get some feeling back in them, get the circulation going—and that's when he noticed the girl wasn't breathing. The girl wasn't breathing! How long had she been like this? He froze and listened, to make sure he wasn't imagining. He watched her to see if her chest was rising or falling. Nothing.

"Hey!" he said, nudging her. "Hey, are you okay?"

"Wha—?" she answered, less than half awake.

Okay, good. She's alive!

"Thirsty," she mumbled, and he reached out from under the tarp for some snow for her to put in her mouth. Then she was back asleep, and he watched her more closely. She was breathing now, he noticed, but her breath was definitely uneven.

"Don't you stop breathing," he whispered. "You're gonna be okay, you hear me?"

A few hours later—hours that felt like years—Jared spotted the first hint of sunlight coming in through the tarp. Not sunrise, not yet, but that early pre-sunrise light that illuminates the clouds.

We did it. We're going to make it through the night.

He peeled out from under the tarp to take a look outside. He reached for his boots and tried to put them on, but he could no longer fit them onto his feet. *That's weird*, he thought. *Why would my boots shrink overnight?*

Then he remembered that edema—swelling—is one of the effects of being at high altitude. While he'd been wearing the boots, they'd compressed his feet and contained the swelling, but once he'd taken them off, apparently they'd puffed up a bit.

Or I have frostbite, he thought. *Or my boots are frozen solid and they're harder to put on. Or all three.*

He knew his Gore-Tex socks would keep out the snow, so he didn't bother with the boots yet. He wanted to have a look around.

Outside their tarp, it was still extremely cold. It looked like about two feet of fresh snow had fallen overnight. It was lighter, more powdery, and less icy than the snow they'd been crossing. But the wind had died down and it was no longer snowing. The storm had cleared! He could see the sunrise making its way over the ridgeline.

The sun lit up the valley below them, and he could see a row of trees. They had nearly made it to the tree line.

They were so close.

Seeing it there—still a walk away, but walkable!—filled him with calm. Despite the cold air, he noticed a fresh warmth radiating from inside him.

They were going to make it.

They were going to be okay.

Three days from now, I'll be at my sister's wedding in North Carolina. In a week, I'll be back at work on the Air Force base in Cheyenne. This is all going to make one hell of a story.

He went back inside to wake the girl.

He knew she hadn't slept well. He'd been awake more or less the entire night, but she had gone in and out of a strange sleep. Her breathing really worried him. Sometimes it would be heavy and rushed; other times, she'd stop breathing altogether—and if he noticed this, he would nudge her again to make sure her breathing would return to normal. Nudging her seemed to help her breathing, but he wasn't quite able to wake her. She seemed to have gone into a trance state.

It must be the exhaustion, he kept telling himself. But he wondered if it was something worse, something more worrisome. Was she having heart trouble? From some of his past research on wilderness first aid and mountain rescue, he knew that the same phenomenon that was causing swelling in his feet could sometimes cause swelling in the heart and lungs—a condition called HAPE, high-altitude pulmonary edema. The change in air pressure forces fluid into the lungs and interferes with breathing. It can be very, very dangerous. There was a similar condition, HACE, where instead of affecting the lungs, the fluid swells into the cerebrum: the brain.

If she was suffering from either of these, then they were in real trouble, and needed to get help soon.

He climbed back under the tarp, where she was curled inside the sleeping bags. He noticed how stale the air was in here, compared to outside, and wondered how much carbon dioxide they'd been breathing all night long.

"Hey, you awake?" he asked.

She mumbled something, but he couldn't make out what she'd said.

"I have great news," he told her. "The storm cleared. I can see the tree line."

She didn't answer.

"It means we're almost back. We're almost safe."

He'd been expecting her to sit up with excitement, and found himself disappointed when she didn't seem to react to his news at all.

"Did you hear me? We're not that far from the tree line. We'll be able to walk there in maybe an hour."

Finally, she rolled toward him.

"No, I don't think so."

He didn't understand what she meant by this.

"Come on; we should get going. There's daylight."

"No. I don't want to walk anymore."

He took a breath.

"Okay. But we have to walk just a little farther and then, really, I think we're safe."

"No," she said, and then bundled herself deeper into the sleeping bags.

What was she thinking?

"I know you're still waking up; I know you're still half-asleep, but maybe you didn't understand: I found the tree line!"

"*You* don't understand," she said. "I've decided not to walk anymore."

She said this with so much calm and so much conviction, it gave him a chill.

"I've had a good life. Now I'm going to wait here for a helicopter or for Jesus." Then she grabbed his hands and looked him in the eye. "Do you know Jesus?"

He couldn't believe what was happening. They had climbed for about twenty hours, almost to safety, survived the night through a raging blizzard, and they were practically there—and now she was giving up.

He wished he remembered her name. After they'd left Mikk for the summit, he didn't have anyone to remind him. Why hadn't he asked her before it was too late—before they'd gone through this whole enormous experience together? He needed to connect with her, and he wanted to say her name.

"Yes," he told her. "I know Jesus. But I am not ready to lie down and wait for him just yet. I've got things to do with my life. We have to get out of here."

"What? What is it you have to do?"

He couldn't believe he was arguing with her about whether or not it was worth fighting to stay alive. He was so shocked to be having this conversation that he didn't know how to answer.

"My sister is getting married this weekend. I have to be there. I'm playing recorder at her wedding."

"Recorder?" The girl sat up for the first time.

"Yeah, it's like a little flute—"

"I know what a recorder is! You play recorder?"

"Yeah. I play lots of things. My family's very musical."

"Like what else do you play?"

"I play French horn. It's like a big trumpet, but bent into a circle."

"Huh." She looked him thoughtfully. "A musical Air Force guy."

He couldn't believe this was what she was interested in talking about right now.

"What else?" she asked.

"What other instruments?"

"No. What else do you have to do with your life?"

"Well, I've got a kickball tournament I'm supposed to be playing in tomorrow. So I guess I have to get down off the mountain for that. And if we die up here, then I'll be AWOL, and that's not cool. So, what do you say? Will you walk off this mountain with me so I can make it to my sister's wedding and play kickball and not be AWOL?"

What was he going to do? If she wouldn't move, then maybe, at least, he could dig her a better shelter. The extra two feet of snow that had fallen overnight meant he would be able to build up and carve out a more thorough ice cave or igloo, somewhere she'd be better protected from the wind and cold.

He left the tarp, scouted out a better spot, and started digging. With the extra depth, he might be able to shield her completely from the wind. And if the snow was strong enough, he might be able to assemble it into a roof, with an air hole, and it would trap in the heat.

How much time will all that take? he wondered. *Digging and building, when they could be climbing to safety.*

He considered whether or not he would really be able to leave her here, sheltered in a snow cave. He knew in his heart that if he left this camp, he would never find it again. The girl would die out here alone, hidden from any possible rescue because of the shelter he was building her. He might as well be digging her a grave.

He imagined how he would feel, knowing he'd left her behind. It would haunt him forever. He imagined what it would be like facing Dan, his friend, who had known her since they were kids. He imagined trying to explain his actions to her parents: "You see, I left her behind because I thought it would be for her own good. She wanted to wait for a rescue." Even he didn't believe it, not for one minute.

He couldn't do it. No way.

He marched back to the shelter where they'd spent the night.

"We're going," he told her forcefully. "You can do this. I'm taking the tarp and the sleeping bags and I'll tear down our little shelter if that's what it takes for you to come with me. But I am not leaving you alone up here. We have to climb down and we have to get to safety. Do you understand?"

"Yes," she said. Her mood seemed to have changed while he'd been gone. "Let's do it."

CHAPTER
FOURTEEN

SEPTEMBER 1, 2010

8:00 A.M.

On Mount Rainier, the trees thin out and then stop growing altogether between 6,500 and 7,500 feet, where the air becomes too scant and the ice, too persistent for any tree to take root. If you see trees on Rainier, then it's safe to say you're below 7,500 feet of elevation.

For a climber who is lost on the mountain, this is good news for a few reasons. First, there are no glaciers—no risk of plunging into a crevasse, no danger of giant seracs cracking and dropping literal tons of ice on your head, no fear of losing your footing and sliding down a 1,000-foot chute before smashing into rocks.

But also, where there are trees, there might be water. And if you can find wood, you might be able to build a fire.

Most important, at a lower elevation, you might run into other people.

Or you might not. Mount Rainier is massive—100 square miles, twice the size of Mount St. Helens, big enough to spawn six distinct rivers. The national park surrounding the mountain takes up 236,381 acres—almost 400 square miles—almost all of it uninhabited: no people, no paths no rescue.

They were climbing down the mountain, yes—but climbing down where? And into what? If they were lucky, maybe they would stumble straight down to the ranger station at Paradise, where they had started their adventure.

If they were unlucky, then they might wind up roaming through countless miles of wilderness.

I want to be lucky, Diane thought. *I will pray to be lucky.*

She had always believed in the power of prayer, certainly, but the past day and especially the past night had confirmed it for her. By the end of the night, she had given up—not given up living, as Jared seemed to assume, but given up pretending that she could control the outcome, could affect God's will. If He wanted her to live, she would. If He had a different plan for her, then that would be her destiny. In the darkest part of the night, she had let herself fall into God's arms, and found great comfort there.

She had spent her whole life growing up with Mount Rainier filling the sky. She knew the native Salish people had called the mountain "Tacoma," which means "the mother of all waters." It was a beautiful image: this giant mountain that is a wellspring for all life.

But she knew, too, that it was a volcano with terrible destructive power.

Life and death.

Relinquishing her control over the last night of her life and her death—turning her fate over to Jesus—that was what had saved her and gave her peace. That was what let her survive the night, and that was the only thing giving her the energy now to keep climbing their way down the mountain toward what they hoped would be survival.

She wanted to live.

Please, Jesus, if it is Your will, please let us live.

They still had to climb down a significant expanse of the glacier before they could make it to the tree line. They had to climb back up, away from the crevasse where they'd camped, and find a way around it in order to continue down. But she felt a bit lighter now, and anyway, the weather was clear and with that came improved visibility. Now they could see across the glacier well enough to chart themselves a course that would thread around the crevasses—the visible ones, anyway. They knew the recent snowfall had brought a new danger: crevasses that might have been easy to see yesterday might now be covered over with a thin blanket of snow. The smooth ground beneath their feet might be hiding a treacherous or deadly fall.

"Hey, I found some more food," Jared said. "Peanut-butter pretzels. You want some?"

"Are you kidding me? Those are my favorite! Where were they?"

"Inside my jacket pocket."

He had lost a glove somewhere while breaking down their camp. They'd spent a few minutes looking for it, but then he decided he didn't want to waste any more time. Since then, he'd been keeping that hand wrapped inside an extra hat and jammed into his coat pocket.

She ate the pretzels joyfully and then considered the fact that this was the last of their food. How long would this handful of pretzels need to sustain them?

She tried to chew more slowly and savor them a little longer.

Jared had overestimated how close they were to the tree line—or maybe he had downplayed the distance intentionally to help get her moving. They had been hiking a few hours already, but a lot of it had been lateral zigzagging instead of climbing down. Now, though, they were closer to the first trees—hardy, scruffy, twisted things—and beneath those, a thick carpet of lush evergreen.

Jared was ahead of her, climbing down.

"Hey, Jared."

He looked up at her.

"What's up?"

She looked around, left and right. She had a hunch, vivid and hard to explain.

"I have a strong feeling that our camp is over there, to the left."

"Camp Muir?" Jared asked.

She nodded. She had a pretty good sense of direction in general, though who could guess whether or not it would be reliable on this mountain after everything they'd been through.

Still, she felt certain—dead certain—she was right.

"Yeah, I'm sure it's this way."

He knew he wasn't aiming them anywhere in particular, except down. He wasn't especially partial, left or right. If she felt strongly about going this way instead of that, then why not?

"Sure," he said. "Let's do it."

This time, Diane led the way.

A half hour later, he called out to her from behind.

"Hey! Look up!"

She squinted, not recognizing or understanding at first what she was seeing: the gray geometric shapes on the mountain above them.

Camp Muir.

CHAPTER
FIFTEEN

Back in time . . .

TO AUGUST 31, 2010

4:00 A.M.

When Dan Claussen decided to turn around and return to Camp Muir instead of keep pushing toward Rainier's summit, he was disappointed not to make it the whole way, but his disappointment wasn't the main thing on his mind. His wife, Amber, was.

His *wife*. They had only been married a few weeks now, and the word "wife" still amazed him. He had a wife!

And that meant he had responsibility. This wasn't like a climb he might have done with his brother Jon, especially when they were younger—those fearless and maybe reckless climbs that brought them close to danger so many times that sometimes he didn't think of danger as dangerous anymore. It was more like a challenge.

But that was different now. Now his first priority was making sure Amber got back to Camp Muir safely.

Amber was a good climber—they had climbed together before—but they both knew she had less experience in the mountains than Dan and, at times, she felt as though she had reached her limit, especially when the weather got worse. She wasn't weak, or out of shape, or a complainer. She knew what she was capable of and was not afraid to let her husband know.

Once they got back down to base camp, he knew she'd be fine.

He felt bad leaving his group behind, but mainly because this climb was going to be something they all did together. Dan had already summited Rainier a few times, and he wanted to do it again—but he didn't have a deep burning urge to do it today. His old coworker, Jared, on the other hand: Jared really wanted to make it to the top. Dan knew it had eaten away at Jared all year that they hadn't summited last summer, and as far as it was possible, Dan wanted to help his friend do it this time.

But it wasn't going to be possible, not today, not for Amber—and if it wasn't possible for Amber, then it wasn't possible for Dan.

The others would be fine, though; Jared had been here before and had logged a lot of climbing experience since then, and Mikk also had experience on the mountain. Climbing Rainier was hard work, but it was a straightforward-enough prospect, at least up the Ingraham Glacier: pick your way carefully around the crevasses following the charted route marked by guides and rangers, take it slow and steady, and get yourself a sunrise selfie at the top. No big deal.

He and Amber got back to Camp Muir around 7:00 a.m. and reunited with their friend Josh. Josh's stomach bug seemed to have passed, and the three of them sat around swapping stories while making a relaxed breakfast.

It was only when another one of their group, Hansen, came

into the cabin, flanked by an entire guided climbing group, that Dan thought to worry.

"What happened?"

Hansen shrugged.

"The altitude."

"All of you? This whole group turned around because of the altitude?"

Hansen told him the altitude had been only one factor in his decision to turn around. The other had been the weather.

Dan exited the cabin and saw that an ominous cloud had dropped over the mountain. He looked up the mountain, wondering if conditions were worse at the summit—but the cloud cover was thick enough that he couldn't see the summit.

A few hours later, someone else was spotted climbing down the glacier toward Camp Muir, and Dan was relieved: things at the summit must not be too bad, after all. *Jared, Mikk, and Diane have probably made it to the summit and are almost back*, he thought.

When that single climber arrived at the camp with no others behind him, Dan was alarmed to discover that it was Mikk—without Jared or Diane.

"They decided to keep going," Mikk explained. "I waited as long as I could, but all my water was frozen and I just couldn't stay out there any more."

"Where was this?" Dan asked.

"It couldn't have been too far from the summit," Mikk said. "It took all I had to stay focused on the way down; I'm pretty sure I even had imaginary phone conversations with my sister and my girlfriend," he laughed, with a hint of worry in his voice.

Dan shook his head, a little worried but half laughing too. *All right, Jared, you crazy fool*, he thought. Jared's willpower was notorious. On the one hand, that meant that of course he would be too obstinate to turn around; Dan should have known that. But on the other hand, that same obstinacy would be the thing that guided Jared and Diane down the mountain.

"They'll be fine," he said, and hoped it was true.

The group waited inside the cabin, playing cards and trying not to worry. But their watches ticked past 1:00 p.m., past 2:00 p.m., and then past 3:00 p.m. They should have been back by now. Even under these conditions, even if they were crawling, they should have been back by now.

"I'm going to go find them," Dan told Amber.

"Dan, no! Not by yourself. Take Hansen with you."

"Hansen, you feel like going for a walk?"

Dan and Hansen strapped on their crampons, roped up, and made their way back up the mountain. When they reached Ingraham Flats, they were met by a pair of mountain guides.

"You guys can't go any farther, it's not safe right now," they told Dan.

"Our friends are out there; they haven't returned from their summit attempt this morning. We are going to find them," Dan told them, as he and Hansen marched right past the guides. If Jared and Diane were climbing down, then eventually they should be able to see them. And if they were in trouble, then maybe Dan and Hansen would be able to help.

But the storm was bad and getting worse. They hadn't gone much past the Flats when Hansen started feeling nauseous again. Dan decided to set up the tent and wait for a bit for Hansen to recover.

How much longer would they wait? Dan didn't know. They couldn't see a thing. Even if Jared and Diane were only a hundred feet away, Dan wasn't sure he'd be able to see them in this weather.

Looking for them was pointless—worse than pointless since now they were also putting themselves at risk. Hansen wanted to keep going up the mountain, but continued to throw up, this time, inside Dan's tent stuff sack.

"Yeah, let's turn around. We need to get you back down to a lower elevation. Who knows, maybe they passed right by us and they're back at Camp Muir eating ramen."

But Jared and Diane weren't back at Camp Muir.

"At what point should we be worried?" Amber asked.

"I think we're at that point," Dan whispered to her.

"Okay, so at what point do we tell the rangers?"

"I think we're at *that* point too."

Dan approached the ranger stationed at the base camp. He thought about that "climbing rescue fee" he had refused to pay, down in Paradise after receiving the $125 ticket for "feeding the wildlife." He felt a bit different about it now that they might need a climbing rescue.

"My friends," he explained to the ranger, "they're still up on the mountain."

A climbing ranger's job is to try to provide climbers with the information they need to stay safe on the mountain. This ranger lived part-time at this base camp, nearly two miles up on the side of the mountain. As part of his job, he had seen Rainier's worst weather. He had rescued people from crevasse falls and avalanches, and he had seen climbers die. And he took Dan very, very seriously.

"It is a beast of a storm out there."

He asked Dan a series of questions, trying to get as many details as he could about Jared and Diane's route, their timeline, their gear, and their experience on the ice. Dan answered the best he could.

"Never? This woman Diane has never done any mountaineering

at all?"

"Not until today, no, sir."

"And the guy she's with, Jared. How many times has he summited the mountain before?"

"Uh, which mountain?"

"This one," the ranger said. "Mount Rainier."

"Yeah—never."

The ranger wrote everything down.

"We can't go out looking for them now—not at night, not in this kind of storm. If your friends are coming back to base camp tonight, they're doing it under their own power."

Dan nodded. This was bad news. There would be no quick rescue. Jared and Diane might walk through the door at any minute; he wouldn't put that past either of them. But he also knew that his friends might be stuck out on the glacier all night long.

The ranger promised to call down to his supervisor at Paradise Visitor Center and begin setting up a search-and-rescue team for the morning.

"If anyone from your party needs to use the satellite phone to call their families or whatever, let me know."

Dan called his brother Jon.

"We might have some trouble up here. I need you to do me a favor."

There were twelve different routes up and down Rainier, and only seven of them passed through Camp Muir. If Jared and Diane had gotten turned around, or if they'd teamed up with another group for their stormy descent, then it was possible they had come down the mountain safely, but on a completely different route.

It's possible they had already made it down to any of the other trailheads—Longmire, Mowich Lake, White River—but didn't have any way to reach Dan or the rest of the group.

That's why Dan wanted his brother to make a call to their old boss, Jared's dad.

The phone rang at the Rund house.

"Hey, Boss. How're you doing? This is Jonathan Claussen."

Jared's dad wasn't used to getting calls this late, especially not from the Claussens.

"Jonathan, how are you? What's going on?"

"Yeah, I was wondering if you've heard anything from Jared?"

Mr. Rund frowned. Why should he have heard from Jared? What were these boys up to?

"I talked to him last week. Why? If you hear from him, tell him to call me. I need his flight details for Caroline's wedding this weekend."

This confirmed for Jon that Jared hadn't come down the mountain or tried to reach his dad—hadn't, in fact, tried to reach anyone who would have contacted his dad. In all likelihood, hadn't tried to reach out to anyone at all. In all likelihood, was still somewhere on Rainier.

Bad news.

"Okay, thanks. Talk to you later!" Jon hung up, leaving Mr. Rund staring at his phone and wondering what was going on.

Around this time, Diane's mom texted Josh's sister, Dana, asking her if she had heard anything from her brother or from the rest of the team. They should have been back to Paradise by now or maybe already on their way home. Dana quickly responded that there was a storm on the mountain, and yes, they were safe in the hardened shelter at the base camp, and were staying on the mountain an extra day to ride out the storm, so they would be a little delayed returning to Duvall.

No one could sleep. They listened to the blizzard rage through the cracks in the stone walls of the hut and thought of their friends on the mountain. Where were they now? They knew that above Camp Muir, there wasn't much shelter from the wind and snow—and the wind and snow were coming on hard. They knew there were caves, geothermal ice caves, up on the summit, and they wondered if—or, at least, hoped that—their friends were hunkered down inside them.

As Josh laid on his bunk, he thought about Diane and Jared, probably freezing to death while they sat there and did absolutely nothing. *This is crazy! There has to be something we can do!* He had seen God perform several miracles in his life up to that point. On this night, he prayed that He would provide one more for his friends. He asked God to keep them safe, give them wisdom, and show them the way down. He prayed like he never had in his whole life. He couldn't stop praying.

On the other side of the hut, Dan thought to himself, *Jared is in the military. And he's so proud; there's no way he'll let himself become a search-and-rescue statistic if there's anything he can do about it.* Dan smiled a little, thinking of his friend's stubbornness and what an asset it might be in this sort of situation. *And Diane is one tough kid too.*

Just rest, he told himself. *Rest, and help them in the morning.*

He stared at the ceiling for a few seconds, and then climbed out of his bunk. He threw on his coat and boots and walked outside to the ranger hut. The ranger was wide awake, still working to organize the search team.

"Hey," Dan said. "Put me to work. Tell me how I can help."

Josh, meanwhile, continued to pray through the night until the break of day, when suddenly he felt the burden was lifted. He stopped praying, somehow feeling it wasn't necessary any longer. He wasn't sure how or why, but he just knew; in his heart, he knew they were either dead or no longer in danger.

By morning, the ranger had lined up a helicopter search-and-rescue team from Fort Lewis–McChord, a joint Army and Air Force Base outside Tacoma. Not all helicopters are capable of flying in the thin air of Rainier's altitude, and this search needed one that could make it all the way to the mountain's 14,411-foot top. Because of budget cuts, the National Park Service didn't have a rescue helicopter of their own, but they could usually call on the Army and their heavy, two-rotor Chinooks whenever they needed to launch a search-and-rescue mission.

Unfortunately, the helicopter and its crew weren't going to be available to them until later in the day.

The team stood outside Camp Muir, gazing across the horizon. They could see nothing except miles and miles of fresh, unbroken snow. Collectively, they had a terrible sinking feeling. They continued their conversation with the ranger, describing Jared and Diane, hoping some bit of information—anything—would help the rescue effort.

"She's wearing a light-blue jacket and black pants," Amber told them. "He's wearing, I think, dark blue. They should be coming down Ingraham Flats."

Josh left the group that was huddled outside the ranger hut and headed to the outhouse. On his way there, he spotted two people climbing up the mountain from below. But they weren't coming from any of the standard routes that led down to Paradise. Instead, they were climbing across the Nisqually Icefall, which people avoid this late in the season.

"Hey, guys!" Josh shouted to his group of friends. "What color jackets were Diane and Jared wearing?"

"Ummm, navy blue and light blue—or teal—I think," Amber replied.

"There are two climbers coming from over there, down to the

right from the Nisqually side. It looks like they are wearing those colors!" Josh yelled jubilantly.

Several hundred yards down, coming from the completely wrong direction, were two climbers wearing what appeared to be light- and dark-blue jackets. The group yelled at the top of their lungs until finally these two climbers heard them, threw their hands into the air, and waved back. It was them; it was Jared and Diane.

CHAPTER
SIXTEEN

SEPTEMBER 1, 2010

10:00 A.M.

Jared sat in the stone hut, holding a Gatorade in one hand and hot chocolate in the other. The girl was nearby, eating peanut butter by the spoonful from a jar.

They felt stunned, exhausted, relieved—and a little bit like celebrities.

"Are you the miracle climbers?" someone wanted to know. "We heard about you. What happened?"

Not long after they had seen Camp Muir—seen it and also been seen by some at the camp—two people started running down to where they were to meet them. They were Josh and Amber, followed quickly by Dan and the others. They all exchanged big hugs, shouted, laughed, and then offered to carry Jared's and Diane's packs the rest of the way.

Jared, who never liked accepting help from others, said, "Absolutely, you can carry my pack."

The remaining walk up to the base camp was simultaneously the longest and shortest of Jared's life. He started recounting details, but he realized he was throwing out details of their experience in whatever order they popped into his head, instead of the order in which it had all occurred. His legs felt strange and he was suddenly enormously tired.

"Dude," Dan asked, "when is the last time you ate?"

They chugged from their buddies' Nalgene water bottles and were lured up the rest of the short climb with the promise of food and hot drinks.

When *was* the last time he ate? He felt his adrenaline starting to drain out of his system; it had been the only thing holding him up for the past day and a half, and without it, he felt more than a little woozy.

"I'll tell you what," he told his friend. "Let me sit down and get some food in me, and then I'll tell you all about it."

But as they were climbing up that last bit, he recalled something important.

"Dan," he whispered, "what's that girl's name?"

Dan laughed so hard he almost fell over. They had just been through this near-death experience together and survived, and the whole time, Jared hadn't known her name.

"It reached a point where it was too awkward to ask," Jared explained, keeping his voice low.

This made Dan laugh harder.

"Diane!" he exclaimed. "Her name is Diane."

A
t Camp Muir, the ranger greeted them and led them into his hut. There, he gave them their first wave of snacks and drinks.

"You two are very, very lucky. I've personally seen people lose their lives out here in conditions that were way less severe than what you survived."

The ranger didn't grill them for details—just asked them how they felt and tried to get a handle on what sort of medical issues they might be experiencing. Other than that, he wanted them to rest and rehydrate, and whenever they were ready to walk down to Paradise. The ranger there would follow up to get information for their complete report.

"So we have to walk down to Paradise, then," Diane said. She was still thinking—hoping—for a ride in a helicopter or on a snowmobile.

Using maps and the ranger's help, they confirmed what they already knew: they had come down the mountain on a different route than the one they had gone up. The Nisqually Glacier, the one they had followed down the mountain, included the Nisqually Icefall and the Nisqually Cleaver, and was a popular route in the winter months, when a deep freeze set in and filled the path with snowpack. But in the summer, this route was mostly unused because, in the words of one ranger, it's a "glacial war zone of rockfall and icefall." Widening crevasses, tumbling seracs, and crumbling rocks and ice make the route treacherous and deadly in the warmer months.

"We tell people not to use any of the Nisqually routes in the late summer. Way too many exposed crevasses."

"You're not kidding about that," Diane said.

"We had a search team about to go out, including helicopters. But to be honest with you, we weren't going to look on Nisqually, not today, anyway. You were so far off any of the main routes that if you hadn't found us, you would probably have been out there at least another night."

Jared and Diane shared a look. They both knew they may not have survived another night. If they hadn't found their own way back to Camp Muir, they might not have come home at all.

The group reunited in the Ranger hut, September 1, 2010. Left to Right: Hansen, Jared, Dan, Josh, Amber, and Diane who is enjoying her peanut butter and the guy she just met.

Now they were back inside the big stone hut, eating what was probably their sixth meal and telling their story for probably the dozenth time.

Jared had expected that the warmth of the hut and a fresh pair of socks would start to bring some feeling back to his numb foot, but he still couldn't feel his big toe. He held it under the light, looking for any visible signs of frostbite. He had never had frostbite—had never even seen it—and didn't know quite what to look for. But he remembered a first-aid class that had taught him that when frozen limbs become flushed with red, that's a good sign—a sign of blood rushing back in. If the limb stays white, that is bad for the opposite reason: blood doesn't rush into dead tissue.

Was his toe more red or more white? Between the blisters, the pruned skin, the grit and dirt, and the poor lighting, he honestly couldn't say for sure. *Something I should keep an eye on*, he thought.

In the midst of all the celebrating, the ranger called Diane's mom.

"It's a miracle! Your daughter is alive!" he exclaimed happily into the phone to Diane's confused mother as she nearly spilled her coffee all over the Starbucks table.

"Why *wouldn't* she be alive? I thought they all spent the night at the base camp shelter?"

"No ma'am. Not your daughter. The route she came down and the storm we had last night—I've seen people perish in much better conditions."

Until then, no one had told her that Diane had spent the night lost on the mountain.

After that call, Diane decided it was important to get back to her parents so she could tell them firsthand what had happened. The rest of the group needed to get moving. All of them were a day behind schedule, with families and jobs waiting for them at home. Jared was going to miss his flight back. He needed to call his boss to let him know of the situation.

So they gathered up their things, said good-bye to the ranger and the rest of the climbers at Camp Muir, and made their way back down to Paradise.

Despite all Jared's fatigue and everything he'd been through, this hike felt easy and light. He was alive! They were alive. It was a clear, sunny day—a rare thing on Mount Rainier—and going down the trail, Jared saw things that he hadn't had a chance to notice during the dark hike up. It was beautiful. When they came off the Muir

Snowfield, they entered an area called Pebble Creek, coursing with water runoff that tumbled down the mountain. Water! What he would have given, a few hours ago, for this water. As they wound down the hairpin switchbacks, they passed through alpine trees and then, finally, meadows full of wildflowers. It was breathtaking. He was so grateful to see it.

Throughout the hike, he and Diane walked close to one another. The group kept asking them questions about their experience, trying to get the details clear in their heads. The two of them shared looks sometimes: they knew that what they had experienced couldn't exactly be put into words. It was something of a secret that the two of them, and only the two of them, would always share.

"We're alive," they seemed to say to each other silently. This feeling kept crashing down on Jared in a hundred different flavors—gratified, relieved, filled with awe and wonder. Some people might take a near-death experience as a reason not to climb mountains at all. But this feeling, this feeling of being alive and appreciating it, this feeling of awe and wonder—that was exactly why people did climb mountains.

He understood that now, more clearly than he ever had.

And Diane understood it too.

They came to the paved trail that makes up the final two miles of the hike to Paradise, and walked down its stone-carved stairs.

The ranger at Paradise was waiting for them. He had them recount their story again—how many times were they going to have to tell this tale today?—and he jotted down notes to make an official report.

"I need you to understand how unbelievably fortunate it is that we are having this conversation with seven climbers today instead of five," he told them all. Then he proceeded to list every single bad decision they had made, any one of which might have led to their death. In addition to lecturing them about climbing in the bad weather, period—let alone, without more experience, more gear, and a working GPS—he reprimanded them for splitting up. "When someone in your team needs to turn around, you all need to turn around. That's what a team is."

the most luxuriant and the most extravagantly beautiful of all the
ine gardens I ever beheld in all my mountain-top wanderings.'
—John Muir, conservationist, 1889

The group back at Paradise, one day later than planned.

He also wanted to make sure they knew that their bad decisions could have affected more lives than their own.

"Today we assembled a team of people to begin looking for you. That means every one of those people were putting their lives at risk too. I've seen rangers—experienced climbing rangers who have summited the mountain many times—wind up in mortal danger because of the poor decisions of inexperienced climbers."

Finally, he softened his tone.

"My real point in all this isn't to make you feel bad. I'm really glad you're alive and healthy. But if you have any plans to do this sort of thing again—if you love these mountains the same way I do—then I'm asking you: please, please respect them. And that means study up: learn to be a safe mountaineer, learn to look out for one another, learn not to put other mountaineers at risk. If you're not willing to do that, then it's better if you stay home."

These were hard words for Jared to hear. But he heard them, and he thanked the ranger for his time and his care.

"Oh, and one more thing," the ranger said. "I noticed none of you paid for your climbing permits on your way in. You each owe us thirty dollars."

Jared and Diane on Muir steps. 'We made it!'

CHAPTER
SEVENTEEN

SEPTEMBER 1, 2010

6:00 P.M.

Diane sat in front of a giant burrito smothered in cheese and enchilada sauce. Her parents sat across the table from her at one of their favorite Mexican places, Ixtapa.

Jared sat next to her.

"I'm still not wrapping my head around all this," her father said. "Maybe you can go through it again one more time?"

Diane wasn't exactly wrapping her head around all of it either. Last night, she had been delirious and maybe close to death, sleeping in the middle of a cracked ice field during a snowstorm. Today, she was wearing a dress, surrounded by ceramic Mexican bowls, vases, and mosaic tiles, eating chips and salsa, and drinking glass after glass after glass of water, trying to quench what seemed like an endless thirst.

She couldn't quite believe she was here.

And the man who had survived this experience with her, the

man who had more than once saved her life, was here with her, sitting beside her, in Ixtapa, in Duvall, wearing khakis and a blue button-down shirt and talking to her parents.

"It's pretty weird," Diane agreed with her father.

Earlier, when they were loading up their cars in the parking lot at Paradise, it was clear to Jared he wasn't going to make his flight. He called his commanding officer in Cheyenne from the backseat of Dan's car to explain what had happened, and he received permission to officially extend his vacation one extra day. That got him a four-day weekend, including Labor Day, and it meant that instead of flying back to Wyoming and then immediately leaving again the following day for his sister's wedding, he would be able to change his flight and fly directly to his sister in Raleigh.

But that also meant he was going to be in Washington an extra day.

"You can stay with me," Diane offered. "I'll have to check with my parents, but, I mean—I owe you at least that, right?"

The climbing team ran through the long, slow trickle of errands they needed to wrap up to finish the trip: returning the rented gear to REI; saying good-bye to Hansen, Josh, and Mikk; and swinging by Mary's to give back all the equipment that Diane had borrowed.

"How did it go?" Mary wanted to know.

"I promise, I'll tell you all about it later," Diane answered. "We've gotta go meet my parents." Jared and Diane had already told their story so many times that day. She didn't know how many more times she could go through it—and she knew she would need to provide at least one more thorough account to her parents.

Then Dan and Amber dropped them off in a parking lot next to a red-roofed building with a stone facade: Ixtapa.

"Mom, Dad—this is Jared; I think you met him at Mary's house when I borrowed her gear. Jared, this is my mom and dad, Denise and Keith."

The funny thing about telling their story is that they had already worked it into something of a routine, taking turns providing details, even finishing each other's sentences. They already knew which details to emphasize and when to pause for dramatic suspense.

This time, Diane decided to ad-lib a new detail: "We slept together!"

Her parents froze and Jared turned as red as the salsa.

"You know, to prevent hypothermia."

"Shared a sleeping bag, she means!" Jared added quickly. "With clothes on. Lots and lots of clothes."

That night, Jared called his dad to let him know he was all right and make sure he knew Jared's flight details, while Diane's mom set up an air mattress in the living room.

"We're so, so glad the two of you are okay," she told him when he was off the phone, and though she had just met him that night, she gave Jared a big hug.

The difference between sleeping on a glacier and sleeping on her bed was about as drastic as Diane would have expected. But that didn't mean she had a restful night. The fears she had faced the night before on the glacier had receded to the back of her brain, and she spent this night wondering, *What does it all mean? What's next?* She'd had a profound, invigorating, shattering experience. How was it going to change her? How would these experiences fit into the rest of her current existence? How would she be the same person, but, at the same time, a different person?

And what about this guy sleeping in the next room—this guy who had arrived so suddenly and profoundly into her life? They had shared a thing that was impossible to explain, something that would connect them, somehow or another, forever.

And tomorrow he was leaving.

Diane awoke a little before sunrise in the bedroom where she had grown up. It was still decorated with so many relics from her childhood and teen years. She didn't live in this house anymore, but in her mind it was impossible not to think of this as "her" room, "her" home.

Yet everything looked a little different today. The room was full of familiar things, but as she looked around, she felt detached from them a bit, one step removed, like she was watching from the outside.

She felt something different.

My life, she thought. *Today I feel my life.* She saw, momentarily, what a fragile and powerful and precious thing it was. She wanted to clutch it with both hands and not let go.

Then she remembered: it was time to take Jared to the airport.

It took forty-five minutes to get to Sea–Tac and to Jared's terminal. They didn't talk much, maybe because it was so early in the morning and maybe because neither one of them knew what to say. What do you say to someone after nearly dying—and then living— on Mount Rainier together?

"It's been really good getting to know you," he said to her at the airport curb.

"Yeah," she agreed. "Obviously."

"We should stay in touch. I mean, we should see each other."

"Yeah," she said.

"Soon."

"Yes. We should."

Then he went into the airport, and a short while later, he boarded his plane and was gone.

Diane felt suddenly disconnected from a new part of herself that she had only just discovered.

A weird thing happened after that: her daily life. She had to go straight from the airport to work. She had already missed a day because of getting lost on the mountain. Her boss was a great mentor and a good friend, who was forgiving and understanding, but Diane didn't want to abuse her generosity, and anyway, there wasn't anything else for her to do. She didn't want to sit around ruminating on her recent trauma, and she didn't especially want to sit around wondering what might or might not happen next with Jared, either.

She drove to the physical-therapy clinic where she was working, parked her car, took the key out of the ignition, and broke down sobbing.

It wasn't Jared. It was everything. The whole enormity of her experience came crashing in all at once. While she and Jared were on the mountain, all their efforts were spent trying to hold everything together. Then, once they'd gotten back to safety, together they had been able to turn their experience into a fun story and make everything seem all right.

It wasn't all right. It wasn't a fun story. She had almost died. She had almost died over and over, in crevasses and in the cold and from thirst and exhaustion. She'd fought for her life and then grown worn down and gave up fighting for her life; she had turned her fate over to God and completely let go, ready to fall backward into His arms.

And now she was in the parking lot at work, expected to go about her old life like nothing had happened, like the world wasn't completely turned inside out.

There was only one person in the world who might understand what she was feeling right now, and she had let him get on a plane and fly out of her life.

What was going to happen?

What was going to happen, she told herself, was that she was going to go to work.

And that's what she did. She got out of the car and walked into her place of employment.

Inside, they all wanted to know what had happened. She'd sent them a quick text message, and now they wanted all the details about the climb and about the man who had saved her. It was hard, at first, trying to step back into this life—this life where these people, her friends, gossiped and traded life advice in between helping patients. It was hard trying to be normal again so quickly.

But she really did love her job—and the normalcy of it started to grow on her, and to soothe her.

"We're going to lose you, aren't we?" her boss asked her.

"What do you mean?"

"I mean this guy, Jared. Seems like a keeper."

The first time Jared called, he was at an organic milk farm and on his way to buy a case of Oreos. His sister Caroline loved Oreos, so they were making her an Oreo wedding cake.

"Hey, do you have my recorder?" he asked. "The little plastic flute I had in my bag on Rainier?"

I know what a recorder is, Jared, Diane thought to herself.

"I can't find it. I think I might've left it at your parents' house."

She told him she hadn't seen his recorder, but that she'd keep an eye out for it.

"Can you ship it to me? You know, overnight delivery? The wedding is tomorrow."

"Are you serious? I don't even know where it is!"

After a brief pause, Jared laughed.

"I'm just kidding! I wanted to call and let you know I was thinking of you."

"I was thinking of you too."

"Let's talk again soon, okay?"

"Yes," she said. "Let's talk again soon."

Diane's summer was coming to an end, and with it, its carefree schedule. She had the job she loved but not much else taking up her time. She was hoping for a chance to see Jared again before the end of September, when she had to return to Spokane, where her life would be overtaken by classes and studying and exams, and little else.

But Jared couldn't meet her in September, he explained, because of mountain biking.

"What?" she asked.

"The ski trails at Winter Park Resort—during the summer, they turn them into these great mountain-bike runs, and I've been going down there as much as I can. But when mountain-bike season is done, I'd love to see you."

"Okay . . . " She wasn't even sure how to respond to this. Did he want to come or didn't he? "So when is 'mountain-bike season' done?"

He flew out to Spokane the first weekend of October, after her classes had started but before they became too intense. Neither one of them were sure how things would go. They had shared a momentous experience, for sure—but what would they be like on their own, without life-and-death experiences surrounding them at all times?

It turned out, they were pretty good together. Diane introduced Jared to her best friend, Brittney.

"Oh," Brittney gushed, "I've heard *so* much about you."

Diane rolled her eyes and grabbed Jared by the arm.

"Let's get out of here."

They rented bikes and rode out to a winery. It was beautiful countryside, and it gave them a chance to talk and catch up, and for the first time, get to know each other face-to-face without the specter of danger looming over them. They swapped stories and jokes, and when they arrived at the winery, they found old World War II planes flying around the vineyards, taking off and landing on a small landing strip across the valley. The two of them sat down on the lawn for a picnic.

There was a moment—or, to be honest, a few moments—where Diane thought Jared might kiss her, but he didn't. And then the moments passed, and they rode back into town.

She wasn't looking for a relationship, she really wasn't. And she definitely wasn't looking for a long-distance relationship! She knew that grad school was going to take up almost all of her time, and she also knew she needed—and wanted—to be selfish with that time.

But she felt a connection to this man and she couldn't deny it. It was a connection she hadn't felt with anyone else, ever before. And thanks to the extraordinary circumstances of how the two of them had met, Diane was pretty sure she wasn't going to feel this kind of connection with anyone else, definitely not in the foreseeable future.

Did he feel it too? She couldn't tell.

"That was a fun weekend," he said when she dropped him off at the airport, giving her a quick hug.

No, she thought as she watched him go. *He probably doesn't.*

They stayed in touch over the next few months. Jared took a few trips with some old friends and went back to see his parents in the Chicago area. Diane might have felt a little stung by how he always seemed to have time for any adventure *except for her*—but the fact was, she was too busy. The first real chance she had to see him again was her winter break, and they agreed to meet up for a ski trip in Breckenridge, Colorado, over New Year's.

"This is my friend Diane," he kept saying, every time he introduced her.

His *friend.*

What am I doing here? she kept thinking. She and Jared were having fun, okay—but more than that, they had a connection that she knew was special.

If he didn't agree, then this was all a waste of her time.

CHAPTER
EIGHTEEN

JANUARY 1, 2011

Jared was having a blast in Breckenridge. It was a great way to ring in the New Year. He loved the skiing, of course—but this was also the first time he had seen Diane in months. She was easy to be around, and fun, but the two of them also shared a powerful connection. The more time they spent together, the more clear it was to him that this connection wasn't only because of the experience they had survived together. It went deeper: they were a really good match for each other.

But . . .

What was he going to do with this girl?

He didn't know what the upcoming year was going to hold for him. His post in Cheyenne had been good for him in a lot of ways—stable, predictable work that allowed him to spend the weekends mountain climbing, most of all. But it was a desk job, and he had never wanted a desk job. He was a fire walker: he thrived on a certain level of adventure and excitement in his life, which was part of why he had signed up for the military in the first place. And now he was looking for a military job that could provide him with some of that stimuli.

The United States had troops deployed all over the world, including several active combat zones—so it was a strange fluke that he wound up stationed in Wyoming. Lucky and unlucky at the same time.

But Jared was in the midst of applying to an Air Force Special Operations program. If he got in, it would change the trajectory of his Air Force career. He would almost certainly wind up overseas—and would very likely find himself in higher-risk situations than the ones he faced in Cheyenne.

He was also on his way to climb the south face of Aconcagua, the mountain peak in Argentina, with Dan's brother Jon, who, true to his form, selected the most difficult side of the mountain from which to make the summit. Aconcagua is 22,841 feet high, the tallest mountain in the world outside of Asia, and far larger than anything he had ever climbed. It was quite literally the biggest challenge he had ever faced—physically, at least. If his experience on Rainier had taught him anything, it was that adventuring at high elevation came with significant risks.

The risks, in fact, were a big part of why he did it in the first place.

But his love of risky adventure meant he was not very good relationship material. He knew this about himself. He wasn't looking to settle down or get married. He was looking to work hard, play hard, advance his career, and have some amazing adventures.

During Diane's New Year's visit to Breckenridge, Jared got a taste of what their life might be like together, and it was great. She was meeting all his friends and they were loving her. She was just as eager as he was to hurl down the steep ski runs, just as keen on staying fit and sharp and challenged. She was so full of joy and enthusiasm, and the two of them saw the world in many of the same ways. Her radiant smile lit up the room unlike that of any person he'd ever met.

He understood that what he had with her was special. He wasn't sure she even knew how special he thought she was. He remembered those first days after Rainier, arriving at his sister's wedding, sunburned and battered and bruised, when his dad had rushed up to him, concerned, at Raleigh–Durham Airport Arrivals and said, "Tell me what happened."

"I met a girl," Jared had answered, going on to recount the adventure of the last forty-eight hours on their ride to his sister's house.

"I am glad we are going to a wedding and not a funeral, Jared!" his father proclaimed. I can't wait to hear more about this ice-cave girl!"

"Diane," Jared said. Even if he didn't know where their relationship was going, he knew that much. "Her name is Diane."

He'd never forget it again.

But Jared also knew the vector his life was on: career-building in the military and mountain climbing all over the world, and all the dangers that came with both. He had no desire to change that vector; it was exactly what he wanted.

So he didn't want to lead her on.

This wasn't a time for him to be getting into a serious relationship. He was twenty-four! His parents hadn't gotten married until they were in their thirties, and that seemed right for him. Our twenties are for figuring out who we are, he told himself, and then building that out. Our twenties are for doing all the things we might not be able to do later, when we're older, when we're married.

But he knew Diane thought about this differently. Her parents had gotten married young, and the prospect of this probably felt much more possible to her. Maybe much more important to her too.

What was he going to do?

She was important to him, and the life he wanted for himself was important to him as well. Did he really have to choose one or the other?

He'd already almost lost her once, in autumn after his trip to Spokane to see her. He'd lost his phone. Actually, he'd lost a few phones, while mountain biking, hiking, and who-knows-what, and at some point during that time period, she was sending messages to him and he wasn't getting them. From her perspective, it seemed like he had vanished—stopped responding—and she took that to mean he wasn't interested anymore.

By the time he realized he had lost Diane's number in his old phone, and that she didn't have his new number either, he immediately tried to reach her on Facebook—only to discover she had shut down her account! He tried to remember how long it had been since they'd been in touch—a week? Two?

Long enough for her to get mad and decide it was time to move on with her life.

He tracked her down, the same way they had first met: through Dan and Amber.

Talking to her then had been a bit of a wake-up call for him: he understood a little more clearly how important this relationship was to her. He knew that if it was important to him too, then he would have to be more attentive to saying so, to making her a part of his life.

But it was also the first time he clearly told her what had been holding him back. It wasn't that he didn't like her or feel a connection with her. It was that, if he was going to be in a relationship with her, then he would want to be sure to do it right, to go all in—and he honestly didn't know if he could make that kind of commitment at this point in his life.

"So what are we going to do?" she had asked him.

That's when they decided on this Breckenridge trip—their first actual vacation together, and a chance to try things out.

Now that they were trying things out, he was more confused than ever. He did feel incredibly strongly about her, but it still didn't change the things he wanted from his life right now.

It all came to a head during those last days in Colorado.

"I'm not your *friend*, Jared. I didn't fly all the way out here because I'm your *friend*."

She was frustrated and it was easy to see why: he had been holding her at bay for almost half a year—not wanting to say no, because he liked and appreciated and probably even loved her—but not wanting to say yes, entirely, either.

Now she wanted to know if he was on board or not.

He needed to be honest with her. He owed her that, and it was the only way they might be able to arrive at whatever it is they wanted together.

What it was, really, was a kind of fear. He wasn't afraid of dangling off rocky cliffs or hurtling down icy ski slopes—and he wasn't afraid of commitment either, not exactly. He had made a commitment to the Air Force without reservation and he had no trouble sticking to it.

What frightened him, he realized, was the idea that a relationship with Diane would start to shut down other possibilities for him, the kinds of adventures that he knew were important to him. If he had a girlfriend—or a wife—would he still be able to climb Aconcagua? Would he someday be able to climb K2 or Everest?

Or would the relationship and all its new responsibilities burden him too much to make those climbs? Would the need to stay tethered to this other person hold him back?

He finally confessed this to her in a way he had never even quite confessed it to himself.

"I love you, Diane. And I don't want to do it halfway."

The way she listened to him and heard him—the way she *understood* him—was another testament to the connection the two of them had.

"I get it," she said. "To be honest, I feel the same way."

"You do?" he asked, shocked.

"Of course I do! I don't want a relationship that holds me back. I don't want a relationship that holds *you* back. I want a relationship that helps both of us forward—that helps us become *more* of who were are. Not less."

He had never thought of it that way.

"I believe we can be that for one another," she continued. "But I need to know if you think that too."

That night, he updated his Facebook status to "In a Relationship." Diane McKenney wasn't just his friend. She was his girlfriend.

The two met up as often as they could, separated by a thousand miles. After Jared returned from Argentina, Diane joined him in Chicago for his friend's wedding and met his parents for the first time. "Jared, she's a keeper," his parents said after they'd heard her singing in the shower.

They traveled to San Francisco and Napa Valley after he finished some training in the area, to Seattle for Easter to meet Diane's extended family, and to Colorado with Jared's family for vacation. Their love for each other grew each time they were reunited.

In August, Jared got the call. It was his commanding officer: "Jared, you've been tasked to deploy to Afghanistan. You'll leave for training in November and you'll be in-country before Christmas."

Jared knew this would be the ultimate test of his and Diane's new relationship.

While Diane would be finishing up her physical-therapy program, he would be literally halfway around the world, in a war zone. It wasn't an ideal way for the two of them to begin building a life together.

But Diane took the news better than he had expected.

"I figured this day would come," she sighed.

Before he shipped out, he did everything he could to spend time with her. They drove together to Jackson Hole, where Jared was climbing the Grand Teton with a group of veterans on September 11, 2011. Then he stayed with her in Portland for a week while she finished up one of her internships, and they explored the Willamette Valley and the Oregon coast, getting closer and enjoying every moment.

He knew this relationship was good.

What he didn't know was his own future.

He tried to imagine the life he was about to begin in Afghanistan, but he couldn't. What would it be like? He didn't have enough frame of reference to be able to picture it clearly. He knew guys who were in-country who had more or less normal lives, essentially working nine-to-five jobs on a military base. But he knew other guys who had been sent out on convoys and into firefights, who had survived explosions, whose jobs were anything but nine-to-five.

How was he supposed to imagine his own future—and Diane's role in it—when his entire next year was so full of unknowns?

There was nothing for them to do but enjoy the time they had together and then hope for the best.

In November, Jared's sister Nadia was getting married in Florida, just a few weeks before Jared was scheduled to deploy. Diane went as Jared's date, of course, and during the ceremony, Jared looked at her with love, remembering how they had met just days before his first sister's wedding. He reached across the table and held her hand.

His dad, officiating the wedding ceremony like he had Caroline's, must have seen it, because he suddenly included them in his speech.

"Well," he said. "I got two of them married off. Only one to go."

It was a good weekend, and it was good feeling like Diane had become a part of his family. He didn't quite know how to tell her this, and he didn't quite know how to figure out what the two of them should do next. He knew he had to go to Afghanistan, and he hoped that when he got back, they would be able to figure things out.

But as she was getting ready to head to the airport Sunday morning, he sensed something wasn't right.

"Are you upset?" he asked her.

"Am I upset? Jared! What do you think?" She broke down crying. "What are we doing? What is the future of this relationship?" She had been expecting him to propose all weekend long. "You're about to deploy. I need to know if we're going to be together, or if I need to move on."

They drove to the airport in tense silence. Her words had hit him like a blow to the chest. He'd thought the two of them were having a good time together, that they were on a really good track. He knew they had decisions to make—but he didn't know it was so urgent.

"Everything's going to be fine," he told her when he dropped her at the airport.

"Is it?" she asked, before disappearing into a crowd of airport security.

He had blown it, and he knew it.

As soon as he got back to Cheyenne, he asked his buddy Eric about engagement rings because Eric had just proposed to his girlfriend. The next day, he was in the jewelry store putting together a ring. He picked it up the day before he left for his training in New Jersey.

"Hey, Diane," he said to her on the phone. "Why don't you meet me in New York City, before I head overseas?" He held his breath, waiting for her reply.

"Why, Jared?"

He didn't know how to tell her without spoiling his surprise.

"Come on, Diane. It'll be the last time we get to see each other for a while."

"Yeah," she said coolly. "And I don't want it to be a waste of time."

"I'm buying you the ticket. Please come. I think it really won't be a waste of your time."

They spent their day touring New York City. They saw a lot of the big sights the city had to offer, including the Statue of Liberty, Ellis Island, the Brooklyn Bridge, the 9/11 Memorial, Central Park, Times Square, the Metropolitan Museum of Art, the Empire State Building, and Broadway. They probably covered as much distance that day as they had on Mount Rainier.

He had done some research and took her to dinner at a fine French restaurant in midtown Manhattan, where, upon entering, he was asked by the hostess if he would like to borrow a sports jacket for the meal, a dress code he must have missed in the fine print on the company's website. They brought course after course after course of food. The whole meal took almost four hours! When the meal was over, they also brought the check: the dinner cost about the same as one month's rent in Cheyenne.

His plan had been to propose to her on the top of Rockefeller Center, but the meal had taken so long, he wasn't sure it was still open. He checked his phone and confirmed it was open until midnight.

"Come on," he told her. "There's somewhere we need to be."

They got to Rockefeller Center with about a half hour to spare—but only then did he learn they stop letting people onto the observation deck at 11:00 p.m. He was too late!

Since Diane didn't know his plan, she didn't sense his inner panic. She enjoyed looking at the Christmas decorations and watching people skate around the outdoor ice rink.

"How about we take a little stroll?" he suggested.

He found them a spot in Central Park with some giant boulders and decided this would be the place.

"Let's climb to the top of one," he suggested. "You know, for some privacy."

They scrambled up the rocks and he thought, *Yes, this seems right.* When they were both at the top, he got down on one knee.

"Diane," he said, "I love you. I want to spend the rest of my life with you. Will you marry me?"

She looked at him with a big smile.

"Yes!" she exclaimed.

Two days later, he left for Afghanistan.

They were married seven months later, a month after Jared returned from his deployment, in Diane's hometown of Duvall, Washington, the town where they had first met. It was a rare day in western Washington: there was no rain, which was great news, since they were having an outdoor wedding.

The Mountain was out that day.

As Diane walked down the aisle holding her father's arm, the song that played was "You Raise Me Up," by Josh Groban:

You raise me up, so I can stand on mountains
You raise me up to walk on stormy seas

I am strong when I am on your shoulders
You raise me up to more than I can be

The reception was catered by Ixtapa, the Mexican restaurant they had visited their first night after Rainier, and their wedding cake was topped with "his and her" mountaineers.

Jared and Diane were married now—but their adventures weren't over. In fact, their adventures were just beginning.

Jared and Diane walking down the aisle, July 14, 2012, in Duvall, WA.

The wedding cake topper: mountaineers!

Jared and Diane with her parents, Keith and Denise.

Jared and Diane with Jared's family. Left to right: brother-in law Allen, sister Nadia, mother Barbara, father Jonathan, sister Caroline and brother-in law Gregory.

The wedding party. Left to right: Gavin Light, Hannah McKenney, Titus Rund, Laura Eldridge, Nicholas Denenberg, Ana Cortez, Jared and Diane, Brittany Johnson, Jon Claussen, Mindy Sanders, Willie Harju, Amber Claussen, Dan Claussen.

Leaving the wedding in a 1940 Ford purchased by Diane's grandfather, Larry McKenney, in 1970 and restored with the help of her father Keith.

CHAPTER
NINETEEN

FALL 2015

They were on Longs Peak, a jagged, 14,259-foot piece of granite in the front range of the Colorado Rockies, a climber's dream. The mountain jutted more than 9,000 feet out of its surrounding landscape and demanded both endurance and technique from its climbers. They were above the tree line, and down to their left as they climbed up was Mills Glacier, a giant chunk of ice that came before the steepest part of the climb.

This was not Diane's first time climbing with Jared since Rainier, not even close. But it was impossible to be on a mountain with him without thinking about that time—especially at this elevation, especially this close to a glacier.

The two of them had collected plenty of experience together since their first adventure, experience in climbing and also experience in living. They had climbed all over the Alps and in Africa, and were planning trips to the Andes, Australia, and the Amazon. They had lived overseas.

Their life, it seemed, was a series of great adventures. But that wasn't quite true, Diane realized. Their life was one single great adventure, and it was ongoing.

They were climbing Longs Peak. Those years ago, when the ranger at Mount Rainier scolded them for their bad decisions on the mountain, he had also challenged them: "If you want to be a mountaineer, then you need to think and act like a mountaineer. You need to be more prepared, more careful, and most of all, you need to remember that the lives at risk aren't just your own."

They had heeded that ranger's advice more than he would ever know.

The sound and feel of her rigid hiking boots made Diane think, invariably, about Rainier. The specter of that mountain had always loomed over her: in her childhood, towering in the skyline—and now, impressing her in a different way. Whenever she was back in Seattle, visiting her family, she would see it and feel again how that mountain had changed her, how it had helped her become who she was today. She felt connected to it: "The Mountain." "The Mother of All Waters." She knew that it had tested her, had dragged her through her worst—and there she had seen herself and understood herself in a deeper way.

There she had also met the man with whom she would build her life.

They approached the Keyhole, the distinctive beginning of the stony ridge that sat at 13,200 feet. Past the Keyhole was exposed, slick rock, and it was all too easy to slip and tumble down hundreds of feet to the granite below. Sixty people had died on this mountain since the opening of Rocky Mountain National Park, and most of those were right here at the Keyhole. One misstep was all it took.

They climbed slowly, with caution, and she understood that this caution didn't make them worse adventurers. It made them better ones.

When she lifted herself, finally, toward the top of the ridge, she stopped to look back and marvel at the route she'd climbed, and that's when she saw:

Jared was missing.

Her heart thumped in her chest.

Where was Jared?

Whenever they climbed, Diane always had a keen sense of Jared—of where he was on the trail ahead or behind her. It wasn't that she was watching him, exactly, not consciously. It was that she had grown to be able to feel his presence.

And now she didn't feel it.

She looked below her at the craggy rocks, jutting up like teeth. There was nothing.

She took a few steps back toward the Keyhole, and scanned the ridge, where the route led down the other side.

Up on a higher route, there he was—safe, safe and looking around for her. When he saw her, he smiled, a big, warm, true, deep smile, and she smiled back.

He feels it too, she realized: the presence and absence. The two of them weren't roped together, not literally, but even from this distance, there was a tether between them, invisible, spiritual. They were connected, and they knew it, and they always would be. And it didn't make them weaker. It made them stronger. It made them better. It made them able to climb higher.

That's what love is.

AFTERWORD

Since meeting, Jared and Diane have climbed many mountains together around the world, completed an Ironman Triathlon, and participated in many other adventure races as teammates. Diane finished the Abbott World Marathon Majors, completing the final marathon of the group in Tokyo in 2017. The couple currently resides in Park City, Utah. On July 28, 2018, along with their good friend Rich Bae, the couple summited Mount Rainier for the first time since August 2010. They could not have asked for better weather.

the most luxuriant and the most extravagantly beautiful of all the gardens I ever beheld in all my mountain-top wanderings."

Rich Bae, Jared, and Diane back on the Muir steps before their summit bid in July 2018.

Diane on the rim of the cone on July 28, 2018. The Columbia Crest summit pictured in the upper left.

Diane and Jared back on Mount Rainier Summit. This time with clear skies and wonderful views!

ACKNOWLEDGEMENTS

Jared and Diane would like to thank the Mount Rainier National Park Service Climbing Rangers for their selfless service and sacrifice. The 2010 Rainier "Chocolate Fox 125" climbing team for their friendship, rescue efforts, and constant prayers during our darkest hours: Dan and Amber Claussen, Hansen Topp, Josh Bresler, and Mikk Kaschko. To Scott Hollmaier and Jon and Dan Claussen, thanks for the inspiration! To Christopher DeWan, we cannot thank you enough! Carolyn Erickson, we love you!

ABOUT THE AUTHORS

DIANE MCKENNEY is an orthopedic physical therapist, devoted wife, long distance runner, mountaineer, and lifelong adventurer. When she is not on a trail with Jared, she can be found helping veterans and athletes recover from their injuries and climb their "mountains."

JARED RUND served for eight years in the Air Force as an active-duty logistics officer, and was twice deployed to Afghanistan. He looks forward to every new adventure that he has the opportunity to experience with Diane by his side. Jared currently runs a real estate investment company in Park City, Utah, and he loves to mountain bike, ski, and climb.

Find more information about the book and authors
at www.strangersinthestorm.com.